Seal of the State of Virginia

CHRONOLOGY AND DOCUMENTARY HANDBOOK OF THE STATE OF

VIRGINIA

ELLEN LLOYD TROVER

State Editor

975.5

WILLIAM F. SWINDLER

Series Editor

1979 OCEANA PUBLICATIONS, INC./Dobbs Ferry, New York

Library of Congress Cataloging in Publication Data

Main entry under title:

Chronology and documentary handbook of the State of Virginia.

   (Chronologies and documentary handbooks of the States; 46)
   Bibliography: p.
   Includes index.
   SUMMARY: A history of Virginia in chronological format with
supporting documents, biographical outlines of prominent citizens, and
a name index.
   1. Virginia—History—Chronology. 2. Virginia—
Biography.   3. Virginia—History—Sources. [1. Virginia
History]   I. Trover, Ellen Lloyd.   II. Series.
F226.5.C47   975.5'002'02   78-26655
ISBN 0-379-16171-0

7.5⁰

Manufactured in the United States of America

TABLE OF CONTENTS

INTRODUCTION ix

CHRONOLOGY (1606-1977) 1

BIOGRAPHICAL DIRECTORY 33

FIRST STATE CONSTITUTION 45

SELECTED DOCUMENTS 55
    Ante-Bellum: Governor's Message, 1849 57
    Post-Bellum: Governor's Message, 1866 83
    Public Education: Report of the
      Superintendent, 1871 123
    Basic Facts 143
    Map of Congressional Districts 144

SELECTED BIBLIOGRAPHY 145

NAME INDEX 147

Virginia/
The Dogwood State

INTRODUCTION

The reception of the first ten volumes in this series was generally gratifying, and not the least was the succession of suggestions from readers — library reference departments, individual scholars, and others — for a wide range of documentary materials which could be added to that section of each volume. These suggestions seemed to the editors to justify an interval in the further preparation of the volumes while a search was undertaken for materials of this type.

The resumption of the series now, with the expanded documents section, hopefully will justify both the expectations of readers and the lengthy hiatus in the completion of the volumes.

As was stated in the introduction to the initial volumes, these are intended to be concise ready references of certain basic data for each state, and a starting point for more extended study as the individual may require. For all too many states, local history and documentary material is not conveniently available for the average citizen, or even for the specialist, and if these volumes may generate interest in certain states in local, comprehensive reference publications which fill in the broad outlines suggested here, the editors can only claim an indirect contribution to state and local history.

The original editorial plan for these *Handbooks* is continued: (1) principal historical events, and representative developments of particular social, economic or political significance, are set out in a chronology; (2) then follows a concise biographical directory of the chief state officers — governors and members of both houses of Congress; (3) the first state constitution, the current text of which is readily available in each state; (4) the collection of documents which is described further in the following paragraph; and (5) a short selected bibliography to direct the reader to more detailed source material.

The chronological and documentary sections are obviously the principal reference aids in each volume. The chronology attempts in outline form to tell the story of the state's development from earliest times to the present. The documents seek to help the reader see this development through the eyes of contemporaries — a traveler observing the state's society at a particular period, a governor summarizing, in his message to the state legislature, the needs of the state at the time, an official explaining the problems of such modern-sounding issues as public education, penal and correctional procedures, or the issues which loomed large at certain eras in the state's history, as canal building, corporation regulation in the "trust-busting" days, the coming of the automobile, women's rights, liquor regulation, and the like.

The difficulty in finding such documents can only impress a researcher with the ephemeral nature of much state history. It may suggest, to state agencies of various types, the importance of seeking out and preserving, perhaps on microfilm or other miniaturized forms, all such documents while they are yet available — just as the chronology section hopefully will inspire historical specialists resident in particular states to fill in the many gaps remaining in many state histories.

Finally, as the editors suggest in the introduction to the first volumes in this series, the fundamental purpose of these *Handbooks* is to guide the user to other sources of information with which he may systematically enrich his knowledge of this state and its place in the American Union.

William F. Swindler
Series Editor

Dobbs Ferry, New York

Sic Semper Tyrannis/
Thus Always to Tyrants

State Motto

CHRONOLOGY

1606   <u>April 10</u>. First charter of the Virginia Company of London passed the Great Seal, authorizing the organizing of commercial colonization effort in Virginia.

<u>November 20</u>. James I issued royal instructions for the government of the new colony.

<u>December 20</u>. Three ships of the Virginia Company under Captain Christopher Newport sailed from London with first group of settlers.

1607   <u>April 26</u>. The ships, the <u>Susan Constant</u>, the <u>Godspeed</u> and the <u>Discovery</u>, made first landfall in Virginia.

<u>May 14</u>. After exploring northern shore of the future James River, settlers landed and began construction of fort at Jamestown Island, later calling site "James His Cittie." The gentlemen chosen in London to govern the colony elected as first president Edward-Maria Wingate.

1608   <u>January 2</u>. Captain John Smith, freed from famous captivity by Powhatan, returned to Jamestown and was charged with capital offense in loss of two companions on his venture. This action typified continuing power struggle amont colony's leaders and was broken off by second voyage of Captain Newport, bringing 100 additional settlers from London.

<u>January 8</u>. Jamestown was destroyed by fire, leaving settlers without shelter or provisions in midwinter.

<u>September 10</u>. John Smith succeeded John Ratcliffe as president of council of the colony and instituted firm leadership which halted disorganization and threatened disintegration of the enterprise . Later this same year, in London, Smith's <u>True Relation of Virginia</u> was published, the first of several of his works broadening interest in and knowledge of the New World.

1609   <u>May 23</u>. Believing that the colony showed promise of permanence, Virginia Company

of London sought and obtained a second
charter, converting itself into joint stock
company and placing colony under "one able
and absolute Governor" in place of the
original council.

August 11. Conversion of Virginia from
experimental outpost to permanent settlement was marked by the arrival of six ships
under Sir George Somers, with more than 200
men, women and children. The ships were
survivors of a storm which had wrecked
others in the flotilla in Bermuda.

1610   May 24. Sir Thomas Gates, first royal
governor under the new charter, published
Divine, Moral and Martial Lawes as a rudi-
mentary code of laws for the colony.

June 10. Discouraged survivors of the
"starving time" of the previous winter,
beset by disease and crop failures,
abondoned Jamestown and started to sail
away. At this moment Lord de la Warr,
Thomas West, arrived with new supplies
from London and the settlers returned to
Jamestown the same day.

1614   April. Chief Powhatan's daughter,
Pocahontas, was married to John
Rolfe in Jamestown. Baptized and
christened Rebeccah, her marriage to
Rolfe brought peace between the
settlers and Powhatan's tribe.

1616   June 2. Sir Thomas Dale, who had governed
the colony since September 1611, sailed for
England with John Rolfe and Pocahontas
and Indian companions to visit the royal
court. Pocahontas died and was buried in
England, but her husband and son returned
to Virginia.

1618   November 18. A third and final charter for
the Virginia Company had been issued March
12, 1612, but in a so-called "Great Charter"
promulgated this day, the colony was authorized to establish a general assembly.
Plans were also being drawn in London for
establishment of a college at Henrico, one
of a number of spreading settlements in the
peninsula area.

1619   July 30. The General Assembly of Virginia,
        the first representative legislative as-
        sembly in British North America, convened
        in the church at Jamestown.

        August 30. A Dutch ship disembarked twenty
        black men from Africa at Jamestown.

1621   December 21. The ship Warwick arrived with
        "an extraordinary choice lot of thirty-
        eight maids for wives." Although women had
        first come to the colony as early as 1608,
        the Virginia Company in 1620 announced a
        plan to send over "100 young maids" a year
        to encourage home building and more per-
        manent settlement inland.

1622   March 22. A carefully planned Indian attack
        on the growing settlements wiped out nearly
        one-third of the 1200 settlers in the Pen-
        insula, including all of the Henrico plan-
        tation which had been intended as the foun-
        dation for a college.

1623   May 9. Discouraged with slow profits from
        Virginia, Privy Council began steps to take
        colony over by creating a commission to in-
        vestigate the Virginia Company.

1624   May 24. The crown's assumption of control
        of the Virginia colony was upheld by the
        courts in London. Although for practical
        purposes this terminated the Virginia Com-
        pany and its charter, the Jamestown set-
        tlers and later the royal colony of Virginia
        insisted that the charters merely expressed
        rights which English subjects continued to
        enjoy as "inalienable."

1625   Estimated population of the colony was
        1,232.

1628   March 10. After a period of uncertainty,
        the General Assembly was revived upon
        instructions from Charles I, and claimed a
        right to meet and draw up legislation there-
        after. This led to continuing disputes over
        division of government power with a series
        of royal governors.

1632   September 4. The legislature, now calling
        itself the "Grand Assembly," undertook a

general revision and modernization of the colony's laws.

1634   Reflecting the steady growth of the colony, eight counties were formally created. James City, Charles City and Elizabeth City were named for members of the royal family, as was Henrico, a Latinized form of Henry. Charles River and Warwick River were named primarily for localities. Warrosquoyoake and Accawmack were Indian names.

1635   April 28. In one of numerous power struggles with royal governors, members of the colonial council (upper house of General Assembly) arrested Sir John Harvey and deposed him as governor.

1639   January 11. Although Harvey obtained a new appointment as governor, his opponents finally secured his dismissal. In appointing Sir Francis Wyatt as his successor, King Charles formally decreed that there should be annual meetings of the General Assembly.

1642   Population of Virginia estimated at 15,300 persons.

New Norfolk, later Nansemond County, created.

1643   March 2. The General Assembly converted 1629 monthly courts to county courts, the administrative offices for the counties. This session also established vestry government for the parishes, with power to elect their own clergymen subject to governor's approval.

1644   April 18. Another Indian uprising, led by Opechancanoe, who planned the 1622 massacre, killed 500 settlers. The attack began a war which lasted until capture of Opechancanoe in October 1646.

1645   Northumberland County, one of many local areas named for English counterparts, established.

November 20. County courts were empowered to try all causes in law and equity, and counties were given local authority to

elect burgesses to lower house of General
Assembly.

1649   October 10. Under the leadership of its
royalist governor, Sir William Berkeley,
the Virginia General Assembly proclaimed
its loyalty to Charles II upon hearing of
the death of Charles I.

1651   Gloucester and Lancaster Counties were
created.

1652   Surry County was created.

March 12. A large naval force sent by
Parliament to compel the colony's submission to the Commonwealth appeared off
Jamestown. Upon an offering of relative-
ly mild terms, a surrender was effected.
Principal effect of the English Revolution was to leave colonial assembly free
to extend its control over local affairs
and local elections.

1653   Westmoreland County established.

1654   New Kent County established.

1656   Rappahanock County established.

1658   April 1. When the new royal governor,
Samuel Matthews, ordered the General
Assembly to dissolve, it demonstrated
the power it had accumulated during the
Commonwealth by compelling a rescission
of the order.

1659   March 7. Upon receiving news of the
death of Oliver Cromwell, the General
Assembly proclaimed itself as the independent authority of government in
the colony.

1660   July 31. Under the Restoration, Sir
William Berkeley received a second appointment as governor of Virginia.
Berkeley's experience under arbitrary
Parliamentary government in England,
and the General Assembly's experience
with independent authority during the
same period, inevitably bred a fundamental clash between them.

1662   Accomack County established.

        March 23. General Assembly revised the
        laws of the colony. Primary purpose
        was to delete "disloyal" legislation
        under the Commonwealth, but its long-term
        effect was to modernize and codify en-
        actments of the past four decades.
        Quarter courts were merged into the general
        court.

1664   Stafford County, named for the Earl of
        Stafford, illustrated the resurgence of
        royalist sympathy in the colony.

1667   April. A severe "hurry cane" struck the
        peninsula, destroying most of the grain
        and killing much of the livestock.

1669   Middlesex County created.

1672   Population of Virginia estimated at 48,000
        persons.

1676   April. Threatened by another Indian up-
        rising, and impatient with Berkeley's
        slow preparations to meet it, a group of
        frontiersmen elected Nathaniel Bacon to
        organize a campaign on their initiative.

        June 23. Bacon's independent action was
        condemned as rebellion by Berkeley, who
        called for a force of colonists to arrest
        Bacon. But several hundred of Bacon's
        followers appeared at Jamestown, where
        Bacon himself took his regular council
        seat. Bacon demanded, and secured, ap-
        proval of a series of reform acts which
        became known as "Bacon's Laws."

        July 30. Berkeley and Bacon reached a
        tentative agreement to join forces against
        the Indians. But once Bacon had left
        Jamestown, Berkeley issued a new call
        for his capture as a rebel. Bacon and his
        men proceeded to Middle Plantation (later
        Williamsburg) and issued a "Declaration
        of the People" denouncing Berkeley and the
        wealthy planters who supported him.

        September 19. Alternately attacking the
        Indians and Berkeley's forces, Bacon

compelled the governor to flee to the
Eastern Shore of the colony. When he
heard that Berkeley planned to return
to Jamestown with an army, Bacon entered
the town and burned it to the ground.

October 16. Bacon died in Gloucester
County of "lice and flux." His rebellion
quickly died out thereafter.

1677   February 20. General Assembly met at
        Berkeley's estate, Green Spring, issued
        pardons for rebels who sought amnesty
        and reenacted many of "Bacon's Laws."
        Supporters of the governor at this ses-
        sion were identified as the "Green Spring
        faction."

1683   September 28. When Berkeley's opponents
        finally effected his recall, Lord Howard
        of Effingham became governor. Conflict
        with the General Assembly continued, how-
        ever, when Effingham sought to recover
        for his office some of the powers assumed
        by the colonial government during the Re-
        volution.

1686   October 20. Robert Beverley, clerk of the
        General Assembly, had made his office the
        nucleus for colonial opposition to the
        governor. Effingham won a major victory
        over the legislature when he obtained
        royal authorization to appoint the clerk.

1693   February 8. The long-frustrated plan to
        establish a college in the colony was
        realized when the Rev. James Blair, a
        powerful leader in church and politics in
        Virginia, received a charter for "Their
        Majesties' Royall College of William and
        Mary in Virginia."

        King and Queen, Norfolk and Princess Anne
        Counties, all reflecting the colony's en-
        thusiastic response to the accession of
        William of Orange and Queen Mary, were
        created. Essex and Richmond Counties, also
        established at this time, reflected the
        rapid growth of colonial settlement through-
        out the tidewater region.

1695   August 8. Foundations for the original
        College building, later to be named the
        Sir Christopher Wren Building, were laid
        in Middle Plantation.

1697   Population for the colony estimated at
        70,000.

1698   October 21. Statehouse at Jamestown burned.
        With the decline of population in and a-
        round this first settlement, it was urged
        that the capital be moved to the newly
        named Williamsburg. This was done the fol-
        lowing year.

1699   April 29. Francis Mackemie, founder of
        Presbyterianism in America, petitioned
        the governor, Sir Francis Nicholson, for
        "freedom of liberty and conscience" in
        the colony. Four years later Nicholson
        published the Act of Toleration to this
        effect.

1700   May 10. This date was announced for the
        official transfer of all court and legis-
        lative business to the new capital of
        Williamsburg.

1702   King William County created.

1703   Prince George County created.

1705   Robert Beverley's History and Present
        State of Virginia published in London.

        October 29. The College building burned,
        with loss of all books and equipment. Re-
        construction began with contribution of
        funds by Queen Anne.

1710   October 25. Colonel Alexander Spotts-
        wood, lieutenant governor, proposed a
        bill which the General Assembly enacted,
        creating courts of oyer and terminer to
        relieve the general court.

1716   August 20. Governor Spottswood led a
        group of planters over the crest of the
        Blue Ridge Mountains. The expedition,
        calling itself "Knights of the Golden
        Horseshoe," dramatized the next step
        of colonization, from the piedmont into

the Shenandoah Valley.

1718   A campaign against pirates led to the capture and execution of Edward Teach (Blackbeard). His head was brought back to Williamsburg.

1721   King George, Hanover and Spotsylvania Counties were created, the latter named for the popular governor.

1724   The Reverend Hugh Jones published his History of the Present State of Virginia in London.

1728   Goochland and Caroline Counties established, the former for the new governor, William Gooch.

       Virginia and Carolina commissioners met and ran a survey of the border between the colonies. The project was publicized later by William Byrd II in his History of the Dividing Line.

1731   Prince William County established.

1734   Orange County, named for the House of Orange, was established.

1735   Amelia County, named for a daughter of George II, was created.

1742   Fairfax and Louisa Counties established. Latter named for youngest daughter of George II.

1743   Frederick County established, named for Prince of Wales, future George III.

       Population of the colony estimated at 130,000.

1744   Albemarle County created, named for Earl of Albermarle.

1745   Augusta County created, named for mother of King George III.

1746   Lunenburg County established, being named for Duke of Lunenburg, one of titles of George II.

1747   April 10. Capitol burned, prompting sug-
            gestions that government be moved westward
            to keep up with population movement. Bur-
            gesses voted to remain in Williamsburg and
            rebuild structure.

            November 6. Ohio Company was formally or-
            ganized, as a land development enterprise to
            consolidate Virginia claims to vast area
            north of the Ohio River and west of province
            of Pennsylvania.

            Chesterfield, Culpeper, Cumberland and
            Southampton Counties established.

1752   Dinwiddie and Halifax Counties established.
            This large number of new counties estab-
            lished in the ten years since 1742 demon-
            strated the steady increase in population
            in the transmontane area of Virginia.

1754   Bedford, Hampshire, Prince Edward and Sus-
            sex Counties were added to the growing list.

            January 16. George Washington, having been
            sent by General Assembly to assess develop-
            ment potential in the Ohio Valley, returned
            to report that French planned to establish
            settlements there in spring.

1755   August 14. Preparing to meet French invas-
            ion challenge in the Ohio Valley, General
            Assembly made Washington commander-in-chief
            of Virginia's armed forces.

1757   Loudoun County established, named for Bri-
            tish commander in French and Indian War.

1758   September 14. General Assembly enacted
            "two-penny act," providing that taxes pay-
            able in tobacco could be paid in cash at
            rate of two pence per pound. This relieved
            planters in times of short crops and high
            prices for tobacco, but burdened clergy
            whose stipends were paid only in tobacco.
            King in Council disallowed the act the next
            year.

1763   In the "Parsons' Case," Virginia clergy
            sued to recover losses in real wages sustained
            before two-penny tax was voided. Court gave
            judgment for the clergy, but Patrick Henry
            persuaded jury to award only nominal damages.

1765   May 29. House of Burgesses protested Stamp
        Act, one of various revenue measures Parli-
        ament devised to recover some costs of
        French and Indian War. Patrick Henry, now
        a Burgess, offered series of resolves chal-
        lenging constitutionality of Stamp Act.

1766   February 8. Northampton county court ruled
        Stamp Act unconstitutional, an opinion that
        had political rather than legal effect.

        Richard Bland published pamphlet, Inquiry
        into the Rights of the British Colonies.

        May 11. A major scandal rocked the colony
        when it was discovered that the accounts of
        the late John Robinson, Speaker of the House,
        were short.

1768   The Virginia Gazette began publishing "Letters
        of a Pennsylvania Farmer," written by John
        Dickinson as a summary of the colonists' con-
        stitutional case in the recent Stamp Act
        controversy.

        April 14. House of Burgesses strongly en-
        dorsed action of Massachusetts legislature
        opposing the Townshend Acts, Parliament's
        alternative revenue plan, and condemned the
        suspension of the New York legislature for
        refusing to bear full cost of British garri-
        sons in that province.

        October 26. Norbourne Berkeley, Lord Bote-
        tourt, arrived in Williamsburg, the first
        royal governor to come personally to the
        colony in a generation. Berkeley was sym-
        pathetic to the colony and personally pop-
        ular, but he became the victim of a conflict
        already in progress.

1769   May 19. When the House of Burgesses main-
        tained opposition to Townshend Acts, Ber-
        keley dissolved them. Burgesses met at home
        of Anthony Hays and formed association to
        oppose the tax measures.

1771   September 25. John Murray, Earl of Dunmore,
        succeeded Berkeley as governor. He was to
        be the last royal governor in Virginia.

1773   March 12. Dissolved once more for acts con-
        sidered seditious, Burgesses met at Raleigh

Tavern under Richard Henry Lee and revived
committee of correspondence to plan common
action with other colonies in opposing Parliamentary acts jeopardizing their claimed inalienable rights.

1774   May 27. After another dissolution, Burgesses
met again at Raleigh Tavern and adopted Lee's
motion to call other colonies to meet in a
Continental Congress to devise means of coun-
tering Parliament's closing the port of Boston
and passing other "intolerable acts."

August 1. An extra-legal convention of specially elected delegates met in Williamsburg to
draft non-importation agreement against Britain,
elect delegates to Continental Congress and organize committees of correspondence in each
county.

1775   Virginia's total population estimated at
550,000.

March 20. Peyton Randolph, moderator of first
convention and president of first Continental
Congress, called second convention in Richmond
to ratify Congress' Declaration of Resolves.
Patrick Henry made famous "liberty or death"
speech.

April 20. Lord Dunmore, convinced that the succession of state conventions were preparing for
revolution, ordered Williamsburg's reserve of
weapons removed from powder magazine and put
aboard British warship in York River.

May 3. Patrick Henry marched on Williamsburg
with company of independent militiamen. Dunmore
halted the threat by arranging to pay for con-
fiscated powder.

June 1. Dunmore recalled General Assembly in
effort to conciliate the colony. But Burgesses
replied with item-by-item rejection of Prime
Minister Lord North's conciliation terms, largely
a paraphrase of Thomas Jefferson's Summary View
published the previous year. A week later, Dunmore and his family took refuge on the warship
in the York River.

July 15. This third Virginia convention formally
declared its succession to the royal government,

assumed the executive as well as legislative power
in the colony, and created a Committee of Public
Safety to put the colony in state of defense.

December 1. Fourth Virginia convention, acting
as provisional legislature, prepared to meet
Dunmore's prospective military invasion of colony.
A week later, provincial troops skirmished with
British forces at Great Bridge and proceeded to
occupy Norfolk as precaution against invasion.

1776 January 1. British fleet bombarded Norfolk and
set it afire. In "scorched earth" rejoinder,
colonial forces burned remaining buildings to
complete the destruction.

May 6. Final state revolutionary convention met
to draft constitution for independent commonwealth of Virginia. Nine days later the convention approved Richard Henry Lee's resolution
instructing delegates to Continental Congress to
declare for independence.

June 12. George Mason's famous Declaration of
Rights was adopted by the convention.

June 28. First Constitution of Virginia
was formally adopted by convention. The
next day Patrick Henry was elected first
governor.

July. Prince Edward Academy, later Hamp-
den-Sydney College, became second center
of higher learning in the new state.

October 7. Thomas Jefferson, a member of
the first session of the state General
Assembly, led movement to undertake complete "revisal" of the laws, preserving
only pre-Revolutionary statutes deemed to
be appropriate to the new Commonwealth.

1778 July 4. Virginia troops under George
Rogers Clark captured Kaskaskia, British
outpost on Mississippi. Confident that
entire area would soon be conquered for
Virginia, General Assembly created
Illinois County as local governmental
unit.

1779 February 25. After difficult winter campaign in which Vincennes, on Wabash River,

was captured, lost and recaptured by Clark,
American control of Northwest Territory
was finally established.

May 9. British fleet entered Hampton Roads
and destroyed Continental army supply depot
on shore.

July 1. Thomas Jefferson became governor.

1780   Optimism of the Revolutionary government
            reflected in steady growth of counties in
            western areas as claimed by Virginia. Ken-
            tucky County, for part of the former Dis-
            trict (later state) of Kentucky, like
            Illinois County was symbol of Virginia
            land claims. Recognition of Common-
            wealth's past was given in counties of
            Powhatan and Fluvanna (latter named for
            Queen Anne), and of new independence in
            counties of Henry, Montgomery and Wash-
            ington, named for Revolutionary leaders.
            Rockingham was named for pro-American
            Marquis of Rockingham, while former
            Dunmore County was renamed Shenandoah.

            April. New government authorized trans-
            fer of state capitol from Williamsburg
            to Richmond, as safer and more central
            location.

            October. British forces returned to
            Hampton Roads and occupied Portsmouth
            as supply base to aid British campaign
            in southern states.

1781   January 5. British invasion of Virginia
            led to capture of new capital of Richmond,
            with government officers barely escaping
            to Charlottesville.

            July. Thomas Nelson became governor, but
            soon joined Washington's staff and was
            succeeded by Benjamin Harrison.

            July 25. Lord Cornwallis, seeking to con-
            quer Virginia and cut off southern sector,
            joined Benedict Arnold's forces in Richmond.
            He then retired toward Portsmouth, beat off
            an American attack near Green Spring and
            elected to take up a defensive position in
            Yorktown.

September 5. Washington transferred his
main army to Virginia and brought York-
town under siege. Cornwallis' hope of
being evacuated by British ships was
lost when French fleet under le Compte
de Grasse drove off the relief fleet in
battle of the Virginia capes.

October 19. With retreat cut off and
French and American forces closing in,
Cornwallis surrendered, virtually ending
War of Independence.

1782   Estimated Virginia population: 567,114.

Liberty Hall Academy, from which later
developed Washington and Lee University,
opened in Lexington.

1783   Thomas Jefferson published his Notes on
the Present State of Virginia.

1784   February 1. The Alexandria Gazette began
publication as first daily newspaper in
Virginia.

March 1. Virginia ceded its western
lands, beyond Ohio River, to United States.

July. Patrick Henry again became governor.

1785   March 28. Concerned at the ineffectiveness
of the new national government, Washington
invited Virginia and Maryland leaders to a
conference at Mount Vernon to settle long-
standing disputes over Potomac River rights.
Progress in this conference encouraged a
less successful Annapolis convention but
led in 1787 to the famous constitutional
convention in Philadelphia.

1786   July. Edmund Randolph became governor.
Two years later he was succeeded by his
counsin, Beverley Randolph, when he resigned to lead movement to codify state
law.

1788   June 26. A convention in Richmond ratified the new Constitution of the United
States. Although the necessary minimum
of nine states had already ratified, the
support of Virginia and New York was a
practical requirement for success of the

new national government.

1789   April 30. George Washington was for-
        mally inaugurated as the first President
        under the new Constitution in ceremonies
        in New York City.

        December 3. Virginia ceded a tract of
        land on the south bank of the Potomac as
        part of "federal district" for new govern-
        ment.

1790   First national census showed 747,610
        population.

1791   Henry Lee became governor. As "Light
        Horse Harry" in the Revolution, he had
        been vigorious leader of new government.

1793   March 4. Washington began second term
        as President.

1794   Robert Brooke became governor.

1796   James Wood became governor.

1798   December 21. General Assembly passed so-
        called Virginia Resolution, condemning
        Alien and Sedition Acts as unconstitutional.

1799   James Monroe became governor. As leader
        of the Jeffersonian "states' rights"
        forces, his election consolidated anti-
        Federalist control in Virginia.

1800   Population: 880,200.

1801   January 27. John Marshall of Virginia be-
        came Chief Justice of the United States.
        His Court over next 35 years shaped Ameri-
        can federalism and bred much antagonism in
        his native state.

        March 4. Thomas Jefferson of Virginia be-
        came President, setting stage for epochal
        confrontation with the Marshall Court.

1802   John Page became governor.

1805   William H. Cabell became governor.

March 4. Jefferson began second term as President.

1806   January 16. Giles County created, named for William B. Giles, rising political leader and future governor.

1807   May 22. Trial of former Vice President Aaron Burr began in Richmond, on general charges of treason. Chief Justice Marshall, as circuit justice, presided. Outcome was inconclusive, and chiefly interesting for President Jefferson's declining a subpoena for his delivery of certain papers.

        June 22. A British frigate attacked an American vessel off Virginia capes. Incidents like these eventually led to War of 1812.

        December 25. Nelson County created, named for Revolutionary War leader.

1808   John Tyler, father of future governor and President, became governor.

1809   March 4. James Madison became President.

1810   Virginia population: 974,600.

1811   James Monroe became governor for second time, but soon resigned to become Secretary of State. His successor, George W. Smith, died in fire in Richmond Theater on December 26, and Peyton Randolph, namesake of Revolutionary leader, became third governor within the year.

1812   James Barbour became governor.

1813   March 4. Madison began second term as President.

1814   William C. Nicholas became governor.

1816   James P. Preston became governor.

        August 19. Dissatisfaction with restricted suffrage in first state constitution led to several meetings in western areas of state demanding new constitution. Staunton and Winchester were sites of two such meetings.

1817   January 25. The University of Virginia,
            first state-supported university in the
            nation, was formally opened in Charlottes-
            ville under guiding hand of its founder,
            Thomas Jefferson.

            March 4. James Monroe, continuing the
            "Virginia dynasty" in government, became
            President.

1819   Thomas Randolph, a son-in-law of Jefferson,
            became governor.

1820   Population: 1,065,366.

1821   March 4. Monroe began second term as
            President. Dominance of national scene by
            Jeffersonian party, rather than absence of
            political issues, led to calling this the
            "era of good feeling."

1822   James Pleasants Jr. became governor.

            January 5. Alleghany County was established.

1825   John Tyler, Jr. became governor.

            July. A second Staunton convention deman-
            ded call for a state constitutional conven-
            tion. Rising western pressure over next
            two years led to General Assembly issuance
            of the call.

1827   William B. Giles became governor.

1829   Constitutional convention opened in Rich-
            mond, presided over by ex-President Mon-
            roe with ex-President Madison chairman of
            important committee on suffrage. Chief
            Justice Marshall was also a delegate. Al-
            though piedmont areas had high hopes of
            broadened franchise, the new constitution
            preserved tidewater dominance.

1830   Population: 1,211,405.

            University of Richmond established.

            John Floyd became governor.

            January 15. Floyd County, named for
            governor, was authorized.

1831   <u>August 21</u>. Nat Turner's rebellion began.
         For several months thereafter, sporadic
         attacks on plantations in Virginia and
         North Carolina kept Virginia militia in
         pursuit of rebel leaders. Turner was
         eventually caught and executed.

1832   Virginia legislature debated bill to abol-
         ish slavery, which eventually fell seven
         votes short of majority needed for passage.

1833   Rappahannock County, named for Indian
         tribe.

1834   Littleton Waller Tazewell elected governor.
         A member of the tidewater elite, his elec-
         tion documented the continued control of
         the state by the old families.

1835   Edgar Allan Poe became editor of <u>Southern</u>
         <u>Literary Messenger</u> in Richmond, one of
         leading American magazines of ante-bellum
         period.

1836   Wyndham Robertson became governor.

         <u>March 8</u>. Clarke County, named for George
         Rogers Clark, was established.

1837   David Campbell became governor.

1838   <u>January 29</u>. Greene County, named for Re-
         volutionary leader Nathanael Greene,
         established.

         <u>March 30</u>. Roanoke County established.

         Medical department of Hampden-Sydney
         College, later to become Medical College
         of Virginia, opened in Richmond.

1839   Virginia Military Institute opened in
         Lexington. Representative of state mili-
         tary academies of its day, it pioneered
         in many areas of military and civil
         engineering.

1840   Population: 1,239,797.

         Thomas W. Gilmer became governor.

1842   <u>January 17</u>. Carroll County established,
         named for Charles Carroll, last surviving

signer of the Declaration of Independence.

First coeducational experiment began at Hollins College, and first women's school, Augusta Female Academy, later became Mary Baldwin College.

1845   February 8. Appomattox County (Indian for "tidal river") was established.

1846   William Smith became governor.

1847   March 9. Highland County was established.

March 13. Arlington County created out of former Alexandria County; named for Duke of Arlington.

1849   John Floyd again became governor.

1850   Population, 1,421,611.

After long agitation another constitutional convention· opened in Richmond. Because piedmont counties demanded new basis for representation, dominant suffrage debate was called "Battle of the Basis."

1851   October 23. New constitution was declared adopted. It represented a substantial broadening of electoral franchise and proportionate weakening of the old tidewater dominance.

Joseph Johnson became governor.

March 21. Craig County established, named for Robert Craig, state political leader.

1855   March 23. Cumberland County created; named for Duke of Cumberland, second son of George II.

1856   Henry A. Wise, a vigorous states' rights spokeman, became governor.

February 16. Wise County authorized.

1858   February 13. Buchanan County created; named for President James Buchanan.

1859   October 16. John Brown arrived at Harper's Ferry in effort to foment slave uprising.

Virginia and Federal troops under Robert
E. Lee suppressed the attempt and Brown was
tried and hanged.

1860   Population on eve of Civil War was 1,596,318.

John Letcher became governor. As Southern
moderate, he had opposed talk of secession
and insisted on union as long as possible.

1861   February 4-13. Virginia participated in
21-state "peace convention" in Washington
to seek ways of avoiding civil war. Meantime, state convention met in Richmond to
prepare for appropriate action if Washington meeting failed.

April 17. After prolonged debate and pres-
sure from other Southern states, Virginia
ultimately acceded to secession demands.
Richmond became capital of the Confederate
States of America. Meantime, anti-seces-
sionists held a convention in Wheeling and
proclaimed a "Restoration Government" under
F. H. Pierpont.

July 21. Battle of Bull Run (Manassas)
resulted in rout of untrained and overcon-
fident Union forces.

August 29. Proposal of western Virginia to
secede and form separate state was consent-
ed to by the "Restoration Government" of
Virginia under Pierpont.

1862   March 9. Battle of Monitor and Merrimac,
world's first ironclad warships, took
place in Hampton Roads.

June 2. Union campaign aimed at capture
of Richmond began with Battle of Seven Days.

August 29. Union forces again defeated
in second Battle of Bull Run.

1863   May 2. Confederate forces suffered fatal
blow in accidental death of Stonewall
Jackson, near Chancellorsville.

June 20. Congress admitted West Virginia
as separate state. For a generation after
Civil War, litigation was carried on over
division of claims and debts of two states.

1864   February. "Restoration Government" called
        constitutional convention in Alexandria.

        May 5. Battle of the Wilderness began
        final Union drive in Virginia. Although
        this and subsequent battles were not de-
        cisive, each resulted in gradual weaken-
        ing of Confederate power.

1865   April 2. Richmond was evacuated, and
        partly burned, as Union forces encircled
        the city.

        April 9. Robert E. Lee surrendered the
        forces of the Confederacy to Ulysses S.
        Grant at Appomattox.

        May 9. "Restoration Government" of Gover-
        nor Pierpont formally recognized by Presi-
        dent Lincoln.

        May 22. Confederate President Jefferson
        Davis imprisoned at Fort Monroe.

1867   March 2. Under first Reconstruction Act,
        Virginia became part of Military District
        No. 1.

        March 13. General John M. Scofield ar-
        rived in Richmond, removed Pierpont as
        governor and installed General Henry H.
        Wells in his place.

        December 3. New constitutional conven-
        tion opened in Richmond, under presidency
        of Judge John R. Underwood. In prolonged
        struggle over franchise, denial of elec+
        toral rights to former Confederates and
        provision of a test oath were made part
        of draft constitution.

1869   January 1. After a year of wrangling, so-
        called Underwood constitution was prepared
        for vote. A "Committee of Nine" -- promi-
        nent state leaders concerned with repres-
        sive features of the draft, organized under
        Schofield, Pierpont and Alexander H. H.
        Stuart to seek division of constitutional
        questions into separate parts: the basic
        document, disfranchisement and the test
        oath.

April 10. President Grant agreed to submission of separate parts of constitution
to vote.

July 6. Underwood constitution was adopted, but disfranchisement and test oath
provisions separately rejected. Gilbert
C. Walker became governor; a New Yorker
who had become a Norfolk banker, he was
the candidate of Richard Mahone, a railroad magnate from the western part of the
state who was to build a powerful Republican machine in Virginia in the next decade.

1870   January 26. Virginia, under the Underwood constitution, was formally readmitted to the Union.

Population: 1,225,163, a loss of a quarter of a million persons in the Civil War
decade.

1871   March 28. Mahone's railroad consolidation
bill was passed by the Walker government.
It required the state to sell off its railroad bonds, except for the Richmond, Fredericksburg and Potomac Railroad, and
cleared the way for Mahone to consolidate
several lines into a new corporation, the
Atlanta, Mississippi and Ohio Railroad
under his presidency.

1872   Virginia Polytechnic Institute founded, as
state's land grant college, at Lexington.

1874   James L. Kemper, ex-Confederate leader,
was selected for governorship by Mahone
to expedite return of state to native con-
servative control. In his inaugural
Kemper promised "readjustment" of heavy
postwar debt fixed by Funding Act of 1871.
This touched of struggle between "Funders"
and "Readjustors" for the next decade.

1878   Mahone's next candidate for governor was
F. W. M. Holliday, who was assumed to be
a "Readjustor." But a legislative bill
for revision of the debt and creation of
a state-supported public school system
was vetoed by the new governor.

1879   A refunding measure approved by foreign
bondholders was finally passed by the

legislature. It substituted tax receiv-
able coupons for direct appropriations
to pay for debts. The measure satisfied
neither Readjustors who wanted greater
relief, nor Northern bondholders who cried
"repudiation."

1880   Population: 1,312,565.

1881   Part of Mahone's railroad empire was orga-
          nized as Norfolk & Western Railroad, to
          bring coal from western part of state to
          make Norfolk major coal exporting center.

1882   Mahone (now U. S. Senator) and Readjustors
          chose William E. Cameron for governor. A
          new debt law limited Virginia's assumption
          of postwar debts to two-thirds of the ori-
          ginal figure, leaving creditors to look to
          West Virginia for the remainder. Con-
          servative reaction to the reform led
          to the decline of "Mahonism" in state
          politics.

1885   Rural unrest led to creation of Farmers'
          Assembly in Richmond, which two years
          later merged with National Farmers' Alli-
          ance. Its chief contribution was an or-
          ganized campaign for argricultural educa-
          tion.

1886   Fitzhugh Lee, nephew of Robert E. Lee,
          was elected governor, ending Mahone's
          Republican regime and returning state to
          Democratic control.

          Collis P. Huntington, industrialist and
          guiding force in Chesapeake & Ohio Rail-
          road, extended C. & O. lines to Newport
          News and constructed shipbuilding and dry-
          dock company which became one of largest
          in United States.

1890   Population: 1,655,980.

          Philip P. McKinney headed Democratic ticket
          in defeating remnants of Mahone machine.
          Stressing Republican reliance on Negro
          votes, McKinney's campaign committed the
          state to efforts to limit the Negro vote.

1894   Walton Act, prepared by State Senator
        M. L. Walton of Page and Shenandoah coun-
        ties, introduced secret ballot but effec-
        tively nullified votes of black and white
        illiterates by system of negative voting
        (striking out names of all candidates but
        those being supported).
        Charles T. O'Ferrall of Rockingham became
        governor, defeating strong Populist op-
        position. At same time, insurgent Tom
        Martin was elected to U. S. Senate, marking
        split in Democratic party between Confede-
        rate veterans and young new leaders.

1898   James H. Tyler, a Bryan silverite, was
        elected governor, marking the high tide
        of agrarian insurgency.

1900   Population: 1,854,980.

1901   June 1. A constitutional convention opened
        in Richmond, with twin objectives of creating
        antitrust agency in state corporation com-
        mission and limiting Negro franchise by va-
        rious qualification tests.

1902   A. John Montague, popular Pittsylvania law-
        yer, won governorship. His program for
        broadened popular reforms in government were
        largely frustrated by opposition of Martin
        forces, which had retired from earlier pro-
        gressive position to build power base among
        conservatives.

        July 15. The new constitution was put into
        effect by ordinance rather than popular
        election. It limited voting rights, cre-
        ated state corporation commission and new
        system of judicial circuits throughout state.

1904   April 25. United States Supreme Court dis-
        missed suit challenging disfranchisement
        provisions of new constitution.

        Cooperative Educational Association organized
        in Richmond to attack long neglect on pub-
        lic education in Virginia and other Southern
        states. The association campaigned for
        new legislative action at all levels of
        education.

1905   Senator Martin's growing political power
        was challenged in reelection campaign in
        which direct primary was invoked to off-
        set machine vote. Martin won and his
        protege, Claude A. Swanson, was elected
        governor.

1906   Sweet Briar College was founded.

1910   Population: 2,061,612

        William H. Mann, leader of prohibition
        forces in state, became governor.

1913   Woodrow Wilson inaugurated as President.

1914   Henry C. Stuart became governor. His
        administration was highlighted by enab-
        ling act which provided for special elec-
        tion establishing prohibition.

1917   Wilson began second term as President.

1918   Westmoreland Davis, wealthy attorney
        and planter from northern Virginia,
        elected governor on anti-machine ticket.

        State Highway Commission created to de-
        velop system to modern roads. Because of
        legislative opposition to Davis, its
        full-time appointments were postponed
        until end of his term.

1920   Population: 2,309,187

1922   E. Lee Trinkle, a regular party candidate,
        was elected governor.

1926   Harry F. Byrd, a rising young political
        leader, was elected governor in a cam-
        paign which opposed highway funding
        through bond issues, the start of Byrd's
        "pay as you go" policy.

1927   April 27. A general reorganization of
        state government, limiting elective of-
        fices to governor, lieutenant governor
        and attorney general, was instituted as
        one of the major constitutional revisions
        of the Byrd administration.

1928   John Garland Pollard, educator and promi-
        nent Protestant lay leader, was chosen

for governor by Democrats to offset Virginia's opposition to Al Smith on national
Democratic ticket.

1929   Colonial Williamsburg, world-famous re-
        storation of 18th-century capital, was
        begun under John D. Rockefeller, Jr.

1930   Population: 2,421,851.

        Virginia Museum of Fine Arts, first
        state museum of its kind in the United
        States, established with support of
        Governor Pollard.

1933   Virginia ratified amendment repealing
        national prohibition and repealed its
        own state law on the subject.

1934   George C. Peery of Tazewell became
        governor. He sought to have legisla-
        ture pass enabling acts to permit parti-
        cipation in New Deal relief programs,
        but conservatives defeated most such
        efforts.

1938   James H. Price of Richmond, a moderate
        New Dealer, became governor. Like
        Governor Peery, he aroused opposition
        of Byrd machine to his plans for state
        participation in New Deal programs.

1940   Population: 2,677,773.

1942   Colgate Darden, Jr. of Norfolk was elected
        governor. Modernization of entire state
        educational system, including quality ed-
        ucation for blacks, was keynote of his
        administration.

1946   William H. Tuck of Halifax, a states' rights
        supporter, became governor. His administra-
        tion was highlighted by "right to work"
        legislation against the closed shop.

1950   Population: 3,318,680.

        Strong challenge to Byrd machine came in
        primary struggle between John S. Battle
        of Charlottesville and Francis P. Miller
        of Arlington. Byrd, with help of state
        Republicans, finally was able to achieve
        Battle's victory for governor.

1954   Another strong challenge to Byrd was the
        gubernatorial contest between Thomas B.
        Stanley, wealthy funiture manufacturer,
        and Theodore R. Dalton, Virginia's leading
        Republican. Byrd's personal intervention
        managed to tip scales to Stanley.

        November 15. Following Supreme Court de-
        cision outlawing segregated public educa-
        tion, state commission headed by State
        Senator Garland Gray submitted report
        which became basis of Byrd's plan of
        "massive resistance."

1955   March 5. Virginia established system of
        tuition grants to finance private segre-
        gated education. This was subsequently
        nullified by Supreme Court.

1956   August 27. "Stanley plan" adopted by
        legislature, providing for closing of
        any schools which were ordered desegre-
        gated by the courts.

1958   J. Lindsay Almond elected governor.
        Former attorney general, he was expec-
        ted to continue program of "massive re-
        sistance."

1959   January 19. State supreme court of ap-
        peals, and U. S. District Court in Nor-
        folk, in separate cases, held state plan
        for closing integrated schools to be un-
        constitutional. Governor Almond, after
        initial defiance, submitted plan for
        "freedom of choice" in selecting schools
        by parents.

1960   Population: 3,966,979

1962   Albertis S. Harrison became governor.
        Treating "massive resistance" as dead
        issue, his administration emphasized sub-
        stantial increases in aid to education
        and development of state's economic re-
        sources.

1966   Mills Godwin, leader of campaign to keep
        Virginia in Democratic column in Lyndon
        Johnson's campaign, became governor. Byrd
        machine had now disintegrated with Senator
        Byrd's death; although his son succeeded
        him as Senator, the other Senate seat was
        won by progressive State Senator William
        B. Spong.

1969   State Commission on Constitutional Re-
        vision undertook comprehensive overhaul
        of 1901 constitution. Under broadened
        state powers provided in revision,
        Governor Godwin secured passage of state
        sales tax and issuances of bonds for
        public improvements.

1970   Population: 4,648,494.

        A. Linwood Holton became first Republican
        governor in 20th century, building his
        victory on growing urban voting strength.

1971   September 14. The American Press Institute
        announced its plans to leave its 25-year-
        old quarters at Columbia in 1974 and to
        move to Reston where it would be able to
        find the space for its expanding needs.

        October 1. The soft coal miners went out
        on strike.

1972   March 14. A Congressional redistricting
        plan following the principle of one-man
        one-vote to a certain extent was approved
        by a three-judge United States court.

        June 23. President Richard M. Nixon an-
        nounced that Virginia was eligible for
        federal relief and recovery funds because
        of the flooding caused by Hurricane Agnes.

1973   February 21. The United States Supreme
        Court reversed a federal district court
        ruling and permitted the institution of
        the 1972 legislative reapportionment plan.
        It contained as much as a 16.4 per cent
        discrepancy between the smallest and the
        largest districts of the House of Dele-
        gates.

        November 6. Governor Mills Godwin, Repub-
        lican, was reelected for a second four
        year term, beginning 1974.

1974   February 18. The Virginia legislature
        passed a mandatory allocation system for
        gasoline. It was based on odd and even
        license plates.

        June 4. Pope Paul VI created a new Dio-
        cese of Arlington.

        June 21. The Department of Health, Edu-
        cation and Welfare accepted the desegre-
        gation plans for the Virginia state
        colleges.

1975   May 2. President Gerald R. Ford crowned
        his daughter Susan, 17, queen of the 48th
        Shenandoah Apple Blossom Festival in Win-
        chester.

        October 3. Japanese Emperor Hirohito
        placed a wreath on the Tomb of the Un-
        knowns at Arlington National Cemetery.

        October 26-27. Egyptian President Anwar
        Sadat spent the night at Williamsburg
        as part of his ten day visit to the United
        States.

1976   January 31. President Gerald R. Ford
        visited Williamsburg.

        June 15. President Ford spoke at the
        Baptist Convention in Norfolk.

        July 11. Queen Elizabeth II of Great
        Britain visited Monticello.

        September 1-3. The Southern Governors
        Conference met at Williamsburg.

        September 6. Democratic Presidential nom-
        inee Jimmy Carter made a campaign visit
        to Norfolk.

        October 23. President Ford, Republican
        Presidential nominee, campaigned in Rich-
        mond.

1977   <u>March 29</u>. Governor Mills Godwin signed
into law a bill revising his state's
death penalty statute. It did away with
the mandatory death penalty for persons
committing murder in the course of rob-
bery, rape or kidnapping and for those
who killed for hire or while serving a
prison sentence. The jury was to decide
upon the death penalty.

<u>July 7</u>. Governor Godwin declared a state
of emergency after hearing testimony from
farmers and agricultural officials that
the state was in the midst of its worst
drought since 1930.

<u>November 8</u>. Lieutenant Governor John
Dalton, Republican, was elected governor
of the state for a four year term beginning 1978.

BIOGRAPHICAL DIRECTORY

This directory of Virginia government leaders is in three parts: The first two parts, in chronological order, list the governors of the colony and the commonwealth respectively, while the third part, in alphabetical order, lists the members of Congress, 1789-1970.

1607	Edward Maria Wingate (President of Council)
1607-1608	John Ratcliffe (President of Council)
1608-1609	John Smith (President of Council)
1609-1610	George Percy (President of Council)
1610	Thomas Gates (Deputy Governor)
1610-1611	Thomas West
1611	Thomas Dale
1611-1614	Thomas Gates
1614-1616	Thomas West
1616-1617	George Yeardley (Lieutenant Governor)
1617-1619	Samuel Argall (Lieutenant Governor)
1619-1621	George Yeardley
1621-1626	Francis Wyatt
1626-1627	George Yeardley
1627-1629	Francis West (President of Council)
1629-1630	John Pott (President of Council)
1630-1635	John Harvey
1635-1636	John West (Deputy Governor)
1636-1639	John Harvey
1639-1642	Francis Wyatt
1642-1652	William Berkeley
1652-1655	Richard Bennett
1655-1658	Edward Digges (President of Council)
1658-1660	Samuel Mathews (President of Council)
1660-1677	William Berkeley
1677-1678	Herbert Jeffries (Lieutenant Governor)
1678-1680	Henry Chichele (Deputy Governor)
1680	Thomas Culpeper
1680-1682	Henry Chichele
1682-1683	Thomas Culpeper
1683-1684	Nicholas Spencer (President of Council)
1684-1688	Francis Howard (Lieutenant Governor)
1688-1690	Nathaniel Bacon (President of Council)

1690-1692 Francis Nicholson (Lieutenant Governor)
1692-1698 Edmund Andros (Lieutenant Governor)
1698-1705 Francis Nicholson (Lieutenant Governor)
1705-1706 Edward Nott (President of Council)
1706-1710 Edmund Jennings (President of Council)
1710-1722 Alexander Spottswood (Lieutenant Governor)
1722-1726 Hugh Drysdale (Lieutenant Governor)
1726-1727 Robert Carter (President of Council)
1727-1740 William Gooch (Lieutenant Governor)
1740-1741 James Blair (President of Council)
1741-1749 William Gooch (Lieutenant Governor)
1749-1751 Thomas Lee (President of Council)
1751   Lewis Burwell (President of Council)
1751-1758 Robert Dinwiddie (Lieutenant Governor)
1758-1768 Francis Fauquier (Lieutenant Governor)
1768-1770 Norbourne Berkeley, Lord Botetourt
1770-1771 William Nelson (President of Council)
1771-1775 John Murray, Lord Dunmore

1777	Patrick Henry	1825	John Tyler, Jr.
1779	Thomas Jefferson	1827	William B. Giles
1781	Thomas Nelson, Jr.	1830	John Floyd
1781	Benjamin Harrison	1834	Littletown W. Tazewell
1784	Patrick Henry	1836	Wyndham Robertson
1786	Edmund Randolph	1837	David Campbell
1788	Beverley Randolph	1840	Thomas W. Gilmer
1791	Henry Lee	1841	John M. Patton
1794	Robert Brooke	1841	John Rutherford
1796	James Wood	1842	John M. Gregory
1799	James Monroe	1843	James McDowell
1802	John Page	1846	William Smith
1805	William H. Cabell	1849	John B. Floyd
1808	John Tyler	1851	Joseph Johnson
1811	James Monroe	1856	Henry A. Wise
1811	George W. Smith	1860	John Letcher
1812	James Barbour	1864	William Smith
1814	William C. Nicholas	1865	Francis H. Pierpont
1816	James P. Preston	1867	Henry H. Wells
1819	Thomas M. Randolph	1869	Gilbert C. Walker
1822	James Pleasants, Jr.	1874	James L. Kemper

1878	F. W. M. Holliday	1926	Harry F. Byrd
1882	W. E. Cameron	1930	John G. Pollard
1886	Fitzhugh Lee	1934	George C. Peery
1890	Philip W. McKinney	1938	James H. Price
1894	Charles T. O'Ferrall	1942	Colgate W. Darden
1898	James H. Tyler	1946	William H. Tuck
1902	Andrew J. Montague	1950	John S. Battle
1906	Claude A. Swanson	1954	Thomas B. Stanley
1910	William H. Mann	1958	J. Lindsay Almond
1914	Henry C. Stuart	1962	Albertis S. Harrison
1918	Westmoreland Davis	1966	Mills Godwin, Jr.
1922	E. Lee Trinkle	1970	A. Linwood Holton
		1974	Mills Godwin, Jr.

Abbitt, Watkins, 1948–
Adams, Thomas, 1778–1780
(Continental Congress)
Alexander, Mark, 1819–
1833
Allen, John J., 1833–1835
Allen, Robert, 1827–1833
Almond, J. Lindsay, 1946–
1948
Archer, William S., 1820–
1836
Armstrong, William, 1825–
1833
Atkinson, Archibald, 1843–
1849
Austin, Archibald, 1817–
1819
Averett, Thomas H., 1849–
1853
Ayer, Richard S., 1870–
1871
Baker, John, 1811–1813
Ball, William Lee, 1817–
1824
Banister, John, 1778–1779
(Continental Congress)
Banks, Linn, 1838–1842
Barbour, James, 1815–1825
Barbour, John S., 1823–1833
Barbour, John Strode, 1881–
1887
Barbour, Philip P., 1814–
1825, 1827–1830
Barton, Richard W., 1841–
1843
Bassett, Burwell, 1805–1813,
1815–1819, 1821–1829
Bayly, Thomas H., 1844–1856
Bayly, Thomas M., 1813–1815
Beale, James M. H., 1833–
1837, 1849–1853

Beirne, Andrew, 1837–1841
Blair, Jacob S., 1861–
1863
Bland, Richard, 1774–1775
(Continental Congress)
Bland, Schuyler O., 1918–
1950
Bland, Theodoric, 1780–
1783
(Continental Congress);
1789–1790
Bocock, Thomas S., 1847–1861
Booker, George W., 1870–1871
Boteler, Alexander R.,
1859–1861
Botts, John M., 1847–1849
Bouldin, James W., 1834–
1839
Bouldin, Thomas T., 1829–
1834
Bowden, George E., 1887–
1891
Bowden, Lemuel J., 1863–
1864
Bowen, Henry, 1883–1885,
1887–1889
Bowen, Rees T., 1873–1875
Brady, James D., 1885–1887
Braxton, Carter, 1775–1776,
1777–1783, 1785
(Continental Congress)
Braxton, Elliot M., 1871–
1873
Breckenridge, James, 1809–
1817
Brent, Richard, 1795–1799,
1801–1803
Brown, John, 1787–1788
(Continental Congress);
1789–1792
Brown, John R., 1887–1889

Browne, Thomas H. B., 1887-1891
Broyhill, Joel T., 1953-
Buchanan, John A., 1889-1891
Burch, Thomas G., 1931-1946
Burton, Clarence G., 1948-1953
Burwell, William A., 1806-1821
Byrd, Harry F., Sr., 1933-1965
Byrd, Harry F., Jr., 1965-
Cabell, George C., 1875-1887
Cabell, Samuel J., 1793-1803
Caperton, Hugh, 1813-1815
Carlile, John S., 1855-1857, 1861
Carlin, Charles C., 1907-1919
Cary, George B., 1841-1843
Caskie, John S., 1851-1859
Chapman, Augustus A., 1843-1847
Chilton, Samuel, 1843-1845
Chinn, Joseph W., 1831-1835
Claiborne, John, 1805-1808
Claiborne, Nathaniel H., 1825-1837
Claiborne, Thomas, 1793-1799
Clark, Christopher H., 1804-1806
Clay, Matthew, 1797-1813
Clopton, John, 1795-1799
Coke, Richard, 1829-1833
Coles, Isaac, 1789-1791
Coles, Walter, 1835-1845
Colston, Edward, 1817-1819
Craig, Robert, 1829-1833, 1835-1841
Critcher, John, 1871-1873
Croxton, Thomas, 1885-1887
Crump, George W., 1871-1873

Daniel, John W., 1885-1910
Darden, Colgate W., Jr., 1933-1935, 1939-1941
Daughton, Ralph H., 1944-1947
Davenport, Thomas, 1825-1835
Davis, Alexander M., 1873-1874
Dawson, John, 1788-1789 (Continental Congress); 1797-1811
Deal, Joseph T., 1921-1929
DeJarnette, David C., 1859-1861
Dezendorf, John F., 1881-1883
Doddridge, Philip, 1829-1832
Douglas, Beverly B., 1875-1878
Downing, Thomas N., 1959-
Draper, Joseph, 1830-1833
Dromgoole, George C., 1835-1841, 1843-1847
Duke, Richard T. W., 1870-1873
Edmunds, Paul C., 1889-1895
Edmundson, Henry, 1849-1861
Eggleston, Joseph, 1798-1801
Ellett, Tazewell, 1895-1897
Epes, James T., 1891-1895
Epes, Sydney P., 1897-1900
Eppes, John, 1803-1811, 1813-1815
Estil, Benjamin, 1825-1827
Evans, Thomas, 1797-1801
Evans, Walter, 1895-1899
Faulkner, Charles J., 1851-1895, 1875-1877
Fishburn, John W., 1931-1933

Fitzhugh, William, 1779-1780
(Continental Congress)
Flannagan, John W., Jr.,
1931-1949
Fleming, William, 1779-1781
(Continental Congress)
Flood, Henry D., 1901-1921
Flood, Joel W., 1932-1933
Flournoy, Thomas S., 1847-
1849
Floyd, John, 1817-1829
Fugate, Thomas B., 1949-1953
Fulkerson, Abram, 1881-1883
Fulton, Andrew S., 1847-
1849
Fulton, John H., 1833-1835
Gaines, William E., 1887-
1889
Garber, Jacob A., 1929-
1931
Garland, David S., 1810-
1811
Garland, James, 1835-1841
Garnett, James M., 1805-1809
Garnett, Muscoe R. H., 1856-
1861
Garnett, Robert S., 1817-
1827
Garrison, George T., 1881-
1883
Gary, J. Vaughan, 1945-
1965
Gholson, James H., 1833-1835
Gholson, Thomas, Jr., 1808-
1816
Gibson, James K., 1870-1871
Giles, William B., 1790-1798,
1801-1815
Gilmer, Thomas W., 1841-1844
Glass, Carter, 1902-1918,
1920-1946

Goggin, William L., 1839-
1841
Goode, John, Jr., 1875-
1881
Goode, Samuel, 1799-1801
Goode, William O., 1841-
1843
Goodwyn, Peterson, 1803-
1818
Gordon, William F., 1830-
1835
Gray, Edwin, 1799-1813
Gray, John C., 1820-1821
Grayson, William, 1784-
1787
(Continental Congress);
1789-1790
Griffin, Cyrus, 1778-1781,
1787-1788
(Continental Congress)
Griffin, Samuel, 1789-1795
Griffin, Thomas, 1803-1805
Hamilton, Norman R., 1937-
1939
Hancock, George, 1793-1797
Hardy, Porter, Jr., 1947-
1969
Hardy, Samuel, 1783-1785
(Continental Congress)
Harris, William A., 1841-
1843
Harris, W. Russell, 1941-1944
Harrison, Benjamin, 1774-1778
(Continental Congress)
Harrison, Burr P., 1946-1963
Harrison, Carter B., 1793-
1799
Harrison, Thomas W., 1916-
1929
Harvie, John, 1777-1779
(Continental Congress)

Hawes, Aylett, 1811-1817
Hay, James, 1897-1916
Haymond, Thomas S., 1849-1851
Hays, Samuel L., 1841-1843
Heath, John, 1793-1797
Henry, James, 1780-1781
(Continental Congress)
Henry, Patrick, 1774-1776
(Continental Congress)
Hill, John, 1839-1841
Holladay, Alexander R., 1849-1853
Holland, Edmund E., 1911-1921
Holleman, Joel, 1839-1840
Holmes, David, 1820-1825
Hooker, James M., 1920-1925
Hooper, Benjamin S., 1883-1885
Hopkins, George W., 1835-1847, 1857-1859
Hopkins, Samuel I., 1887-1889
Hubard, Edward W., 1841-1847
Hungerford, John P., 1811, 1813-1817
Hunter, Robert M. T., 1837-1843, 1845-1861
Hunter, W. Godfrey, 1895-1897, 1903-1905
Jackson, Edward B., 1820-1823
Jackson, George, 1795-1797, 1799-1803
Jackson, John G., 1813-1817
James, R. Abraham, 1920-1921

Jefferson, Thomas, 1775-1776, 1783-1785
(Continental Congress)
Jennings, W. Pat, 1955-1965
Johnson, James, 1813-1820
Johnson, Joseph, 1835-1841, 1845-1847
Johnston, Charles C., 1831-1832
Johnston, John W., 1870-1883
Johnston, Joseph E., 1879-1881
Jones, James, 1819-1823
Jones, John W., 1835-1845
Jones, Joseph, 1777-1778, 1780-1783
(Continental Congress)
Jones, Walter, 1797-1799, 1803-1811
Jones, William A., 1891-1918
Jorgensen, Joseph, 1877-1883
Kerr, John, 1813-1817
Kidwell, Zedekiah, 1853-1857
Lamb, John, 1897-1913
Langston, John M., 1890-1891
Lankford, Menalcus, 1929-1933
Lassiter, Francis R., 1907-1909'
Lawson, John W., 1891-1893
Leake, Shelton T., 1845-1847
Lee, Arthur, 1781-1784
(Continental Congress)
Lee, Francis L., 1775-1780
(Continental Congress)
Lee, Henry, 1777, 1785-1788
(Continental Congress); 1799-1801
Lee, Richard B., 1789-1795
Lee, Richard H., 1774-1780
(Continental Congress);
1789-1792

Lee, William H. F., 1887–1891
Leffler, Isaac, 1827–1829
Leftwich, Jabez, 1821–1825
Leigh, Benjamin W., 1834–1836
Lester, Posey G., 1889–1893
Letcher, John, 1851–1859
Lewis, Charles S., 1854–1855
Lewis, John F., 1870–1875
Lewis, Joseph, Jr., 1803–1817
Lewis, Thomas, 1803–1804
Lewis, William, 1817–1819
Libbey, Harry, 1883–1887
Love, John, 1807–1811
Loyall, George, 1833, 1837
Lucas, Edward, 1833–1837
Lucas, William, 1839–1841, 1843–1845
Machir, James, 1797–1799
Madison, James, 1780–1783, 1786–1788 (Continental Congress) 1789–1797
Mahone, William, 1881–1887
Mallory, Francis, 1837–1839
Marsh, John O., 1963–
Marshall, James W., 1893–1895
Marshall, John, 1799–1800
Martin, Elbert S., 1859–1861
Mason, Armistead T., 1816–1817
Mason, James M., 1837–1839
Mason, John Y., 1831–1837
Mason, Stevens T., 1794–1803

Maxwell, Lewis, 1827–1833
Maynard, Harry L., 1901–1911
Mayo, Robert M., 1883–1884
McCarty, William M., 1840–1841
McComas, William, 1833–1837
McCoy, William, 1811–1833
McDowell, James, 1846–1851
McKenney, William R., 1895–1896
McKenzie, Lewis, 1870–1871
McKinley, William, 1810–1811
McMullen, Fayette, 1849–1857
Meade, Robert K., 1847–1853
Mercer, Charles T., 1817–1839
Mercer, James, 1779–1780 (Continental Congress)
Mercer, John F., 1782–1785 (Continental Congress); 1792–1794
Meredith, Elisha E., 1891–1897
Millson, John S., 1849–1861
Milnes, William, Jr., 1870–1871
Montague, Andrew J., 1913–1937
Moore, Andrew, 1789–1797; 1804–1809
Moore, Robert W., 1919–1931
Moore, Samuel M., 1833–1835
Moore, Thomas L., 1820–1823
Morgan, Daniel, 1797–1799
Morgan, William S., 1835–1839
Morrow, John, 1805–1809
Morton, Jeremiah, 1849–1851
Nelson, Thomas, Jr., 1775–177
(Continental Congress)

Nelson, Thomas M., 1816-1819
Neville, Joseph, 1793-1795
New, Anthony, 1793-1805
Newman, Alexander, 1849
Newton, Thomas, Jr., 1801-1829
Newton, Willoughby, 1843-1845
Nichols, John, 1793-1801
Nicholson, W. Cary, 1799-1804
O'Ferrall, Charles T., 1884-1893
Otey, Peter J., 1895-1902
Page, John, 1789-1797
Page, Mann, 1777 (Continental Congress)
Page, Richard, 1799-1801
Parker, Josiah, 1789-1801
Parker, Richard, 1849-1851
Parker, Richard E., 1836-1837
Parker, Severn E., 1819-1821
Patton, John M., 1830-1838
Paul, John, 1881-1883
Paul, John, Jr., 1922-1923
Perry, George, 1923-1929
Pegram, John, 1818-1819
Pendall, James, 1817-1820
Pendleton, Edmund, 1774-1775 (Continental Congress)
Pendleton, John S., 1848-1849
Pennypacker, Isaac S., 1837-1839, 1845-1847
Platt, James H., Jr., 1870-1875
Pleasants, James, 1811-1822

Poff, Richard H., 1953-1969
Porter, Charles H., 1870-1873
Powell, Alfred H., 1825-1827
Powell, Cuthbert, 1841-1843
Powell, Levin, 1799-1801
Powell, Paulus, 1849-1859
Preston, Francis, 1793-1797
Preston, William B., 1847-1849
Pridemore, Andrew L., 1877-1879
Pryor, Roger A., 1859-1861
Quarles, Julian M., 1899-1901
Randolph, Edmund J., 1779-1782 (Continental Congress)
Randolph, John, 1799-1813, 1815-1817, 1819-1827
Randolph, Peyton, 1774-1775 (Continental Congress)
Randolph, Thomas M., 1803-1807
Rhea, William F., 1899-1903
Richmond, James B., 1879-1881
Riddleberger, H. H., 1883-1889
Rives, Francis E., 1837-1841
Rives, William C., 1823-1829, 1832-1834, 1836-1845
Rixey, John F., 1897-1907
Roane, John, 1827-1831
Roane, John J., 1831-1833
Roan, William H., 1815-1817
Robertson, A. Willis, 1933-1965
Robertson, John, 1834-1839
Robeson, Edward J., Jr., 1950-1959
Rutherford, Robert, 1793-1797

Samuels, Green B., 1839-1841
Satterfield, David E., 1937-1945
Satterfield, David E. III, 1965-
Saunders, Edward W., 1906-1920
Scott, William L., 1967
Seddon, James A., 1845-1847, 1849-1851
Segar, Joseph E., 1862-1863
Sener, James B., 1873-1875
Shaffer, Joseph C., 1929-1931
Sheffey, David, 1809-1817
Slemp, Campbell, 1903-1907
Slemp, Campbell B., 1907-1923
Smith, Arthur, 1821-1825
Smith, Ballard, 1815-1825
Smith, Howard W., 1931-1967
Smith, John, 1801-1815
Smith, John A., 1873-1875
Smith, Meriwether, 1778-1782 (Continental Congress)
Smith, William, 1821-1827
Smith, William, 1841-1843, 1853-1861
Smyth, Alexander, 1816-1825
Snodgrass, John F., 1853-1854
Southall, Robert G., 1903-1907
Spong, William B., 1965-1971
Stanley, Thomas B., 1946-1953
Steenrod, Lewis, 1839-1845
Stephenson, James, 1809-1811
Stevenson, Andrew, 1821-1834

Stowell, William H. H., 1871-1877
Stratton, John, 1801-1803
Strother, George F., 1817-1820
Strother, George F., Jr., 1851-1853
Stuart, Alexander H. H., 1841-1843
Stuart, Archibald, 1837-1839
Summers, George W., 1841-1845
Swanson, Claude A., 1893-1906 1910-1933
Swoope, Jacob, 1809-1811
Taliaferro, John, 1811-1813, 1824-1831, 1835-1843
Tate, Magnus, 1815-1817
Taylor, John, 1792-1794, 1803, 1822-1824
Taylor, Robert, 1825-1827
Taylor, William, 1843-1846
Taylor, William P., 1833-1835
Tazewell, Henry, 1794-1799
Tazewell, Littleton W., 1800-1801, 1824-1832
Terry, William, 1871-1873, 1875-1877
Thomas, Christopher Y., 1874-1875
Thompson, George W., 1851-1852
Thompson, Philip R., 1801-1807
Thompson, Robert A., 1847-1849
Thorp, Robert T., 1896-1897
Tredway, William M., 1845-1847
Trezvant, James, 1825-1831
Trigg, Abram, 1797-1809
Trigg, G. F., 1885-1887
Trigg, John J., 1797-1804
Tuck, William M., 1953-1969
Tucker, George, 1819-1825
Tucker, Henry St. G., 1815-1818

Tucker, Henry St. G.,
1889-1897
Tucker, John R., 1875-1887
Turnbull, Robert, 1910-1913
Tyler, David G., 1893-1897
Tyler, John, 1817-1821,
1827-1836
Upton, Charles H., 1861-
1862
Van Swearingen, Thomas,
1819-1822
Venable, Abraham, 1791-1799,
1803-1804
Venable, Edward, 1889-1890
Waddill, Edward, Jr., 1890-
1891
Walker, Francis, 1793-1795
Walker, Gilbert C., 1875-
1879
Walker, James A., 1895-1899
Walker, John, 1780
(Continental Congress);
1790
Wampler, William C., 1953-
1955, 1967-
Washington, George, 1774-
1775
(Continental Congress)
Watson, Walter A., 1913-1919

Whaley, Kellian V., 1861-
1863
White, Alexander, 1789-1793
White, Francis, 1813-1815
Whitehead, Joseph, 1925-1931
Whitehead, Thomas, 1873-1875
Whitehurst, G. William, 1969-
Willey, W. Thomas, 1863-1871
Williams, Jared, 1819-1825
Wilson, Alexander, 1804-1809
Wilson, Edgar C., 1833-1835
Wilson, Thomas, 1811-1813
Wise, George D., 1881-1889
Wise, Henry A., 1833-1844
Wise, John S., 1883-1885
Wise, Richard A., 1898-1900
Withers, Robert E., 1875-
1881
Woodrum, Clifton A., 1923-
1945
Woods, James P., 1919-1923
Wythe, George, 1775-1777
(Continental Congress)
Yost, Jacob, 1887-1889
Young, William A., 1897-1900

FIRST STATE CONSTITUTION

THE CONSTITUTION OF VIRGINIA—1776 * [a]

BILL OF RIGHTS

A declaration of rights made by the representatives of the good people of Virginia, assembled in full and free convention; which rights do pertain to them and their posterity, as the basis and foundation of government.

---

* Verified from " Ordinances passed at a General Convention of Delegates and Representatives from the Several Counties and Corporations of Virginia, Held at the Capitol in the City of Williamsburg, on Monday, the 6th of May, A. D. 1776. Reprinted by a Resolution of the House of Delegates, of the 24th February, 1816. Richmond: Ritchie, Trueheart & Duval, Printers. 1816." pp. 3-6.

" The Proceedings of the Convention of Delegates for the Counties and Corporations in the Colony of Virginia, held at Richmond Town, in the County of Henrico, on the 20th of March, 1775. Re-printed by a Resolution of the House of Delegates, of the 24th February, 1810. Richmond: Ritchie, Trueheart & Du-val, Printers. 1816." 8 pp.

" The Proceedings of the Convention of Delegates for the Counties and Corporations in the Colony of Virginia held at Richmond Town, in the County of Henrico, on Monday the 17th of July 1775. Reprinted by a Resolution of the House of Delegates, of the 24th February, 1816. Richmond: Ritchie, Trueheart & Du-Val, Printers. 1816." 116 pp.

" The Proceedings of the Convention of Delegates held at the Capitol, in the city of Williamsburg, in the Colony of Virginia, On Monday, the 6th of May, 1776. Reprinted by a Resolution of the House of Delegates, of the 24th February, 1816. Richmond: Ritchie, Trueheart & Duval, Printers. 1816." 86 pp.

" Ordinances passed at a General Convention of Delegates and Representatives, from the several Counties and Corporations of Virginia, held at the Capitol in the City of Williamsburg. On Monday, the 6th of May, Anno-Dom. 1776. Reprinted by a Resolution of the House of Delegates, of the 24th February, 1816. Richmond: Ritchie, Trueheart & Du-Val, Printers. 1816." 19 pp.

[a]This Declaration of Rights was framed by a Convention, composed of forty-five members of the colonial house of burgesses, which met at Williamsburgh May 6, 1776, and adopted this Declaration June 12, 1776.

This constitution was framed by the convention which issued the preceding Declaration of Rights, and was adopted June 29, 1776. It was not submitted to the people for ratification.

Section 1. That all men are by nature equally free and independent, and have certain inherent rights, of which, when they enter into a state of society, they cannot, by any compact, deprive or divest their posterity; namely, the enjoyment of life and liberty, with the means of acquiring and possessing property, and pursuing and obtaining happiness and safety.

Sec. 2. That all power is vested in, and consequently derived from, the people; that magistrates are their trustees and servants, and at all times amenable to them.

Sec. 3. That government is, or ought to be, instituted for the common benefit, protection, and security of the people, nation, or community; of all the various modes and forms of government, that is best which is capable of producing the greatest degree of happiness and safety, and is most effectually secured against the danger of maladministration; and that, when any government shall be found inadequate or contrary to these purposes, a majority of the community hath an indubitable, inalienable, and indefeasible right to reform, alter, or abolish it, in such manner as shall be judged most conducive to the public weal.

Sec. 4. That no man, or set of men, are entitled to exclusive or separate emoluments or privileges from the community, but in consideration of public services; which, not being descendible, neither ought the offices of magistrate, legislator, or judge to be hereditary.

Sec. 5. That the legislative and executive powers of the State should be separate and distinct from the judiciary; and that the members of the two first may be restrained from oppression, by feeling and participating the burdens of the people, they should, at fixed periods, be reduced to a private station, return into that body from which they were originally taken, and the vacancies be supplied by frequent, certain, and regular elections, in which all, or any part of the former members, to be again eligible, or ineligible, as the laws shall direct.

Sec. 6. That elections of members to serve as representatives of the people, in assembly, ought to be free; and that all men, having sufficient evidence of permanent common interest with, and attachment to, the community, have the right of suffrage, and cannot be taxed or deprived of their property for public uses, without their own consent, or that of their representives so elected, nor bound by any law to which they have not, in like manner, assembled, for the public good.

Sec. 7. That all power of suspending laws, or the execution of laws, by any authority, without consent of the representatives of the people, is injurious to their rights, and ought not to be exercised.

Sec. 8. That in all capital or criminal prosecutions a man hath a right to demand the cause and nature of his accusation, to be confronted with the accusers and witnesses, to call for evidence in his favor, and to a speedy trial by an impartial jury of twelve men of his vicinage, without whose unanimous consent he cannot be found guilty; nor can he be compelled to give evidence against himself; that no man be deprived of his liberty, except by the law of the land or the judgment of his peers.

Sec. 9. That excessive bail ought not to be required, nor excessive fines imposed, nor cruel and unusual punishments inflicted.

SEC. 10. That general warrants, whereby an officer or messenger may be commanded to search suspected places without evidence of a fact committed, or to seize any person or persons not named, or whose offence is not particularly described and supported by evidence, are grievous and oppressive, and ought not to be granted.

SEC. 11. That in controversies respecting property, and in suits between man and man, the ancient trial by jury is preferable to any other, and ought to be held sacred.

SEC. 12. That the freedom of the press is one of the great bulwarks of liberty, and can never be restrained but by despotic governments.

SEC. 13. That a well-regulated militia, composed of the body of the people, trained to arms, is the proper, natural, and safe defence of a free State; that standing armies, in time of peace, should be avoided, as dangerous to liberty; and that in all cases the military should be under strict subordination to, and governed by, the civil power.

SEC. 14. That the people have a right to uniform government; and, therefore, that no government separate from, or independent of the government of Virginia, ought to be erected or established within the limits thereof.

SEC. 15. That no free government, or the blessings of liberty, can be preserved to any people, but by a firm adherence to justice, moderation, temperance, frugality, and virtue, and by frequent recurrence to fundamental principles.

SEC. 16. That religion, or the duty which we owe to our Creator, and the manner of discharging it, can be directed only by reason and conviction, not by force or violence; and therefore all men are equally entitled to the free exercise of religion, according to the dictates of conscience; and that it is the mutual duty of all to practise Christian forbearance, love, and charity towards each other.

THE CONSTITUTION OR FORM OF GOVERNMENT, AGREED TO AND RESOLVED UPON BY THE DELEGATES AND REPRESENTATIVES OF THE SEVERAL COUNTIES AND CORPORATIONS OF VIRGINIA

Whereas George the third, King of Great Britain and Ireland, and elector of Hanover, heretofore intrusted with the exercise of the kingly office in this government, hath endeavoured to prevent, the same into a detestable and insupportable tyranny, by putting his negative on laws the most wholesome and necessary for the public good:

By denying his Governors permission to pass laws of immediate and pressing importance, unless suspended in their operation for his assent, and, when so suspended neglecting to attend to them for many years:

By refusing to pass certain other laws, unless the persons to be benefited by them would relinquish the inestimable right of representation in the legislature:

By dissolving legislative Assemblies repeatedly and continually, for opposing with manly firmness his invasions of the rights of the people:

When dissolved, by refusing to call others for a long space of time, thereby leaving the political system without any legislative head:

By endeavouring to prevent the population of our country, and, for that purpose, obstructing, the laws for the naturalization of foreigners:

By keeping among us, in times of peace, standing armies and ships of war:

By effecting to render the military independent of, and superior to, the civil power:

By combining with others to subject us to a foreign jurisdiction, giving his assent to their pretended acts of legislation:

For quartering large bodies of armed troops among us:

For cutting off our trade with all parts of the world:

For imposing taxes on us without our consent:

For depriving us of the benefits of trial by jury:

For transporting us beyond seas, to be tried for pretended offences:

For suspending our own legislatures, and declaring themselves invested with power to legislate for us in all cases whatsoever:

By plundering our seas, ravaging our coasts, burning our towns, and destroying the lives of our people:

By inciting insurrections of our fellow subjects, with the allurements of forfeiture and confiscation:

By prompting our negroes to rise in arms against us, those very negroes whom, by an inhuman use of his negative, he hath refused us permission to exclude by law:

By endeavoring to bring on the inhabitants of our frontiers the merciless Indian savages, whose known rule of warfare is an undistinguished destruction of all ages, sexes, and conditions of existence:

By transporting, at this time, a large army of foreign mercenaries, to complete the works of death, desolation, and tyranny, already begun with circumstances of cruelty and perfidy unworthy the head of a civilized nation:

By answering our repeated petitions for redress with a repetition of injuries: And finally, by abandoning the helm of government and declaring us out of his allegiance and protection.

By which several acts of misrule, the government of this country, as formerly exercised under the crown of Great Britain, is TOTALLY DISSOLVED.

We therefore, the delegates and representatives of the good people of Virginia, having maturely considered the premises, and viewing with great concern the deplorable conditions to which this once happy country must be reduced, unless some regular, adequate mode of civil polity is speedily adopted, and in compliance with a recommendation of the General Congress, do ordain and declare the future form of government of Virginia to be as followeth:

The legislative, executive, and judiciary department, shall be separate and distinct, so that neither exercise the powers properly belonging to the other: nor shall any person exercise the powers of more than one of them, at the same time; except that the Justices of the County Courts shall be eligible to either House of Assembly.

The legislative shall be formed of two distinct branches, who, together, shall be a complete Legislature. They shall meet once, or oftener, every year, and shall be called, *The General Assembly of Virginia*. One of these shall be called, *The House of Delegates*, and consist of two Representatives, to be chosen for each county, and for the district of West-Augusta, annually, of such men as actually reside in, and are freeholders of the same, or duly qualified according to law, and also of one Delegate or Representative, to be chosen annually for the city of Williamsburgh, and one for the borough of Norfolk, and a Representative for each of such other cities and boroughs, as may hereafter be allowed particular representation by the legislature; but when any city or borough shall so decrease, as that the number of persons, having right of suffrage therein, shall have been, for the space of seven years successively, less than half the number of voters in some one county in Virginia, such city or borough thenceforward shall cease to send a Delegate or Representative to the Assembly.

The other shall be called *The Senate*, and consist of twenty-four members, of whom thirteen shall constitute a House to proceed on business; for whose election, the different counties shall be divided into twenty-four districts; and each county of the respective district, at the time of the election of its Delegates, shall vote for one Senator, who is actually a resident and freeholder within the district, or duly qualified according to law, and is upwards of twenty-five years of age; and the Sheriffs of each county, within five days at farthest, after the last county election in the district, shall meet at some convenient place, and from the poll, so taken in their respective counties, return, as a Senator, the man who shall have the greatest number of votes in the whole district. To keep up this Assembly by rotation, the districts shall be equally divided into four classes and numbered by lot. At the end of one year after the general election, the six members, elected by the first division, shall be displaced, and the vacancies thereby occasioned supplied from such class or division, by new election, in the manner aforesaid. This rotation shall be applied to each division, according to its number, and continued in due order annually.

The right of suffrage in the election of members for both Houses shall remain as exercised at present; and each House shall choose its own Speaker, appoint its own officers, settle its own rules of proceeding, and direct writs of election, for the supplying intermediate vacancies.

All laws shall originate in the House of Delegates, to be approved of or rejected by the Senate, or to be amended, with consent of the House of Delegates; except money-bills, which in no instance shall be altered by the Senate, but wholly approved or rejected.

A Governor, or chief magistrate, shall be chosen annually by joint ballot of both Houses (to be taken in each House respectively) deposited in the conference room; the boxes examined jointly by a committee of each House, and the numbers severally reported to them, that the appointments may be entered (which shall be the mode of taking the joint ballot of both Houses, in all cases) who shall not continue in that office longer than three years successively, nor be eligible, until the expiration of four years after he shall have been out of that office. An adequate, but moderate salary shall be settled on him, during his continuance in office; and he shall, with the advice of a Council of State, exercise the executive powers of government, according to the laws of this Commonwealth; and shall not, under any pretence, exercise any power or prerogative, by virtue of any

law, statute or custom of England. But he shall, with the advice of
the Council of State, have the power of granting reprieves or pardons, except where the prosecution shall have been carried on by the
House of Delegates, or the law shall otherwise particularly direct;
in which cases, no reprieve or pardon shall be granted, but by resolve
of the House of Delegates.

Either House of the General Assembly may adjourn themselves
respectively. The Governor shall not prorogue or adjourn the Assembly, during their sitting, nor dissolve them at any time; but he
shall, if necessary, either by advice of the Council of State, or on
application of a majority of the House of Delegates, call them before
the time to which they shall stand prorogued or adjourned.

A Privy Council, or Council of State, consisting of eight members,
shall be chosen, by joint ballot of both Houses of Assembly, either
from their own members or the people at large, to assist in the administration of government. They shall annually choose, out of their
own members, a President, who, in case of death, inability, or absence
of the Governor from the government, shall act as Lieutenant-Gov-
ernor. Four members shall be sufficient to act, and their advice and
proceedings shall be entered on record, and signed by the members
present, (to any part whereof, any member may enter his dissent) to
be laid before the General Assembly, when called for by them. This
Council may appoint their own Clerk, who shall have a salary settled
by law, and take an oath of secrecy, in such matters as he shall be
directed by the board to conceal. A sum of money, appropriated to
that purpose, shall be divided annually among the members, in proportion to their attendance; and they shall be incapable, during their
continuance in office, of sitting in either House of Assembly. Two
members shall be removed, by joint ballot of both Houses of Assembly, at the end of every three years, and be ineligible for the three
next years. These vacancies, as well as those occasioned by death or
incapacity, shall be supplied by new elections, in the same manner.

The Delegates for Virginia to the Continental Congress shall be
chosen annually, or superseded in the mean time, by joint ballot of
both Houses of Assembly.

The present militia officers shall be continued, and vacancies supplied by appointment of the Governor, with the advice of the Privy-
Council, on recommendations from the respective County Courts; but
the Governor and Council shall have a power of suspending any
officer, and ordering a Court Martial, on complaint of misbehaviour
or inability, or to supply vacancies of officers, happening when in
actual service.

The Governor may embody the militia, with the advice of the Privy
Council; and when embodied, shall alone have the direction of the
militia, under the laws of the country.

The two Houses of Assembly shall, by joint ballot, appoint Judges
of the Supreme Court of Appeals, and General Court, Judges in
Chancery, Judges of Admiralty, Secretary, and the Attorney-General,
to be commissioned by the Governor, and continue in office during
good behaviour. In case of death, incapacity, or resignation, the
Governor, with the advice of the Privy Council, shall appoint persons to succeed in office, to be approved or displaced by both Houses.
These officers shall have fixed and adequate salaries, and, together

with all others, holding lucrative offices, and all ministers of the gospel, of every denomination, be incapable of being elected members of either House of Assembly or the Privy Council.

The Governor, with the advice of the Privy Council, shall appoint Justices of the Peace for the counties; and in case of vacancies, or a necessity of increasing the number hereafter, such appointments to be made upon the recommendation of the respective County Courts. The present acting Secretary in Virginia, and Clerks of all the County Courts, shall continue in office. In case of vacancies, either by death, incapacity, or resignation, a Secretary shall be appointed, as before directed; and the Clerks, by the respective Courts. The present and future Clerks shall hold their offices during good behaviour, to be judged of, and determined in the General Court. The Sheriffs and Coroners shall be nominated by the respective Courts, approved by the Governor, with the advice of the Privy Council, and commissioned by the Governor. The Justices shall appoint Constables; and all fees of the aforesaid officers be regulated by law.

The Governor, when he is out of office, and others, offending against the State, either by mal-administration, corruption, or other means, by which the safety of the State may be endangered, shall be impeachable by the House of Delegates. Such impeachment to be prosecuted by the Attorney-General, or such other person or persons, as the House may appoint in the General Court, according to the laws of the land. If found guilty, he or they shall be either forever disabled to hold any office under government, or be removed from such office *pro tempore*, or subjected to such pains or penalties as the laws shall direct.

If all or any of the Judges of the General Court should on good grounds (to be judged of by the House of Delegates) be accused of any of the crimes or offences above mentioned, such House of Delegates may, in like manner, impeach the Judge or Judges so accused, to be prosecuted in the Court of Appeals; and he or they, if found guilty, shall be punished in the same manner as is prescribed in the preceding clause.

Commissions and grants shall run, "*In the name of the Commonwealth of Virginia*," and bear test by the Governor, with the seal of the Commonwealth annexed. Writs shall run in the same manner, and bear test by the Clerks of the several Courts. Indictments shall conclude, "*Against the peace and dignity of the Commonwealth.*"

A Treasurer shall be appointed annually, by joint ballot of both Houses.

All escheats, penalties, and forfeitures, heretofore going to the King, shall go to the Commonwealth, save only such as the Legislature may abolish, or otherwise provide for.

The territories, contained within the Charters, erecting the Colonies of Maryland, Pennsylvania, North and South Carolina, are hereby ceded, released, and forever confirmed, to the people of these Colonies respectively, with all the rights of property, jurisdiction and government, and all other rights whatsoever, which might, at any time heretofore, have been claimed by Virginia, except the free navigation and use of the rivers Patomaque and Pokomoke, with the property of the Virginia shores and strands, bordering on either of the said rivers, and all improvements, which have been, or shall be made thereon. The western and northern extent of Virginia shall, in all other respects, stand as fixed by the Charter of King James I. in the year one thousand six hundred and nine, and by the public treaty of peace between the Courts of Britain and France, in the year one thousand seven hundred and sixty-three; unless by act of this Legislature, one or more governments be established westward of the Alleghany mountains. And no purchases of lands shall be made of the Indian natives, but on behalf of the public, by authority of the General Assembly.

In order to introduce this government, the Representatives of the people met in the convention shall choose a Governor and Privy Council, also such other officers directed to be chosen by both Houses as may be judged necessary to be immediately appointed. The Senate to be first chosen by the people, to continue until the last day of March next, and the other officers until the end of the succeeding session of Assembly. In case of vacancies, the Speaker of either House shall shall issue writs for new elections.

SELECTED DOCUMENTS

Because, as in so many Southern states, the Civil
War marked the turning point in the state's history,
the two first documents selected for Virginia are
peculiarly appropriate and revealing.

The first, taken from the governor's message to
the General Assembly in 1849, includes a supplemental
report on the status of slavery in several border and
Northern states as perspective for legislation in
Virginia, where the Jeffersonian tradition of gradual
elimination of slavery was occasionally revived in
the legislature.

The second, taken from the governor's message of
1866, is a dramatic survey of the destruction wrought
by the war and the challenges facing the state, not
entirely disposed of in the present century.

The last document, excerpts from the First Annual
Report of the Superintendent of Public Instruction
of 1871, is concerned with the quality of post war
education in Virginia.

Document 1

MESSAGE

I welcome you, with great pleasure, to the capitol, and offer you my congratulations upon the condition in which you will find the general interests of the commonwealth. Notwithstanding the fears expressed by many lest the liberal spirit evinced in the more recent legislation of the state, touching the improvement of roads and canals, would embarrass our finances, the reports I herewith transmit to you from the several departments, will shew that our condition is sound and prosperous. Indeed, there is every thing in it to vindicate the wisdom of the legislature, and to gratify the friends of a judicious but liberal system of internal improvement. It will be, I am sure, gratifying to you, and to the people at large, to know that Virginia has at her command ample means to discharge all her subsisting public debt, with the exception of a very small and inconsiderable sum. If it were thought desirable to-morrow to wipe out the public debt, a sale at par of her profitable and interest-paying stocks would effect it. This present subsisting debt amounts to $7,541,294 11. The annual interest and dividends received by the state amount to $430,752 08; shewing that the stocks yielding this sum are worth, at par, $7,179,200, or about the amount of the public debt; that is, within $362,000 of our present indebtedness. There is, however, an additional sum of $6000,000, which, under existing laws, may be called for out of the treasury, and about $5,000,000 of which will, it is thought, be certainly demanded in the course of a few years; hence this sum, although not now a subsisting debt, will become so, and ought, therefore, to be taken into the estimates of our liabilities. This view shews the precise condition of our financial situation, and is fully sustained by the reports and documents which will be laid before the legislature. The state, it is true, has guarantied loans, to a considerable amount, for various incorporated companies, which securityship some have regarded a part of the public debt; but this is unquestionably an error, for a knowledge of the resources and the prospects of the companies, whose bonds have been guarantied, will satisfy all that they are, or will ultimately be, amply able to pay their bonds, as, up to this time, they have always done the interest on them.

This exposition is a cheering one to all, but to none more so than the friends of internal improvements, for which the debt has been mainly created. However, whilst it shews the perfect capacity of the commonwealth to manage her present debt without inconvenience, it also shews the necessity of the greatest prudence and circumspection on the part of the legislature, to avoid such increase of our indebtedness as may result in future embarrassment and additional taxation. Nothing ought to be more cautiously avoided, or earnestly deprecated by the advocates of the recent liberal system of improvement than such a result. I would recommend, therefore, that, except such sums as are necessary to carry on the great works already begun, or such as are essentially necessary to contribute to their success and profit, no farther appropriation should be made for the present out of the treasury. I make this recommendation with the greater confidence, because I believe the success of a permanent and wise system of internal improvements depends upon it.

If any thing can ever restore to Virginia that pecuniary and commercial ascendancy which she once possessed in the confederacy, it must be the consummation of the system of internal improvements she has already embarked in, and the completion of the truly great works already commenced. To endanger the system, or to impede the prosecution of those works, is to strike a fatal blow at the resuscitation of the commonwealth; and nothing would be so effectual for this, as a lavish expenditure of public money upon insignificant projects, from which the state at large could never receive any benefit.

The great works of internal improvement, already undertaken and so generously sustained by the public funds and public credit, together with one or two proposed but not yet determined upon, are calculated to develop very fully the resources of the state, and to swell the tide of her commercial prosperity to its utmost limits. The entire energies of the commonwealth should be devoted to their completion, but in such a way as to avoid embarrassment and to escape onerous taxation. That this can be effected by the prudence and wisdom of the legislature, I have no doubt.

It is now reduced almost to an axiom, that the greatest commercial prosperity in the Atlantic States, is only attainable by a connection with the valley of the Mississippi; and hence, from Massachusetts to Georgia, we see almost every state along the sea-coast, competing anxiously and earnestly with each other, for the shortest, cheapest and safest communication.

The commercial ascendancy of Virginia was at one period of our history undisputed; her natural advantages of navigable streams, climate and soil, gave it to her. Trusting to these, we have neglected those artificial means, which could alone secure it to us permanently; and therefore the commerce, which once whitened with its sails our seaports, has almost disappeared from our waters. The example set us by our neighbors at the North is one of wisdom, and deserves our most earnest attention. In spite of a bleak climate and sterile soil, they have, by a judicious policy, afforded such facilities to intercommunication and trade, that commerce with her golden tides has filled the land with plenty, prosperity and wealth. Our natural advantages remain still the same; they are unequalled by any Atlantic state; and whilst it is now probably too late to divert the commerce of the Atlantic cities from its present channels; still it is in the power of demonstration to shew that a vast deal of what we have unwisely lost, can be regained, and that we can still secure a fair division of that commercial wealth and power which is now monopolized by the North.

Situated about midway between the northern boundary of the United States and the Gulf of Mexico, we escape in a great degree the rigors of the northern winters, and the scorching heat of the South. Our eastern border upon the river Potomac and the Chesapeake bay, is dotted with harbors unsurpassed in safety and capacity. The fleets of the whole earth could ride safely at anchor within them. Our western border is washed for several hundred miles by the Ohio river, and at other points along it, the rich region of Kentucky and the fertile valley of the Tennessee are of easy access. Besides this, the country lying between the eastern and western boundaries, of which I speak, is unsurpassed for its fertility and the variety of its products. Minerals of every description are to be found of the most superior quality, and in quantities absolutely inexhaustible, whilst the earth in which they are embedded, unlike other mineral regions, is of the most desirable character for husbandry. Let this country be penetrated by improvements connecting our seaports with the Ohio, with Kentucky and the valley of Tennessee, and it will infuse a spirit of enterprize into the population, which must, in a short time, fully develop all of our resources.

The topography of the country is most favorable for the completion of these great connecting lines. From tide-water to the Mississippi river at Memphis, there is no mountain barrier interposing a serious difficulty to the construction of a railroad, whilst the region traversed by it is inferior to none of the same extent, for mineral and agricultural resources, upon the continent of North America. The valley of the Tennessee, one of the most magnificent of all those washed by the waters of the West, the annual commerce of which is worth thirty-five millions of dollars, will find in this road an outlet for its rich products to the Atlantic. And a cargo of merchandize, landed at Norfolk or Richmond, would be safely transported to the city of Memphis, ready for distribution upon those mighty waters, in less than ten days. The "Virginia and Tennessee" railroad will effect this great object, when it shall be finally completed; and it affords me great pleasure to say, we are warranted in the belief that it will be prosecuted with energy and despatch.

The James river and Kanawha canal, having for its object the connection of tide-water with the Ohio river has for a good many years been generously sustained by appropriations of public money; and, although it has met with strong opposition, it still maintains itself steadfastly in the approbation of well informed reflecting men. The results to Virginia, which are to flow from its completion, will strike the mind, upon a little reflection, as really stupendous. I have no doubt but that the commerce passing through this canal will rapidly build up the towns of Virginia, to the magnitude of the first American cities, and will rescue us in a great measure from the miserable consequences of our past apathy and inaction.

The effects upon the prosperity and destiny of New York, produced

by the completion of the Erie canal opening the commerce of the
lakes to that city, are perfectly familiar to every one; the daily increasing importance of it, is also quite as well understood. Without the
Erie canal, the city of New York would have been second still to Philadelphia. Great as the advantages of this work unquestionably are;
those of the James river and Kanawha canal are undoubtedly superior.
It possesses the striking advantage of lying five degrees south of the
great northern work, and therefore, free from the ice which obstructs
the navigation there, for so large a proportion of the year. It touches
the Ohio river, far south of any water communication from the Atlantic whatever; and at a point, south of which there can be across the
country no water connection. It will, after the first of November,
command all the trade of a great part of Ohio, Kentucky, Indiana, Illinois and Missouri—and most probably, of those regions lying still
higher up towards the sources of the Missouri and Mississippi; for,
after that period, it is unsafe to send produce north, in the direction of
Boston, New York or Philadelphia. A striking and peculiar advantage presented by this line, is its continuity. There is no necessity
whatever for transhipment. We will see canal boats, laden at the falls
of St. Anthony or Council Bluff discharging their cargoes at Lynch-
burg, Richmond and Norfolk. The extent and fertility of the region
through which this work will pass, is unsurpassed by any accessible
country within the territories of the United States. Superadded to
this, the rivers, canals and railroads, emptying into and resting upon
the Ohio and Mississippi, will bring from the remote interior, which in
every direction they penetrate, their contributions, to swell still higher
the rich tide of commerce, flowing through the heart of the commonwealth. The trade in Indian corn, which has recently sprung up, and
is increasing with such surprising rapidity between Europe and America, will be almost monopolized by this line; and will of itself, presently, build up and sustain a great city. Norfolk must be the point
for its shipment, for it can reach there and be sent away, without the
injury which it is sure to sustain from detention at the more southern
points. Indeed, this line will monopolize, in a great measure, the transportation of all the principal articles of food, which are produced in
the Mississippi valley for consumption in our Atlantic States and in
Europe. It is a fact universally known, that provisions of every kind
suffer injury from the climate during their transit by New Orleans and
through the Gulf.

We have seen what the commerce of the lakes has done for the
states of Massachusetts and New York; but the country which supplies it, sinks into comparative insignificance, when looked at by the
side of that I have just described. These are some, probably the
most striking, but only a very few of the reasons which present themselves to the mind in behalf of this great enterprize. To elaborate the
subject would require a volume. I earnestly recommend the steady,
energetic prosecution of the work to its completion.

The South-west is already provided with a great work—the central
line accomplishes all that is necessary, or that can be effected for the
country through which it passes. The Louisa railroad is wending its

way slowly, but most certainly to the banks of the Ohio. The Baltimore and Ohio railroad, together with the Chesapeake and Ohio canal, provide our northern border with every facility of transportation to market.

It has been frequently proposed and very strongly urged, to construct a railroad from some point on this side of the Blue Ridge to the Ohio river at Parkersburg. It would seem as if even-handed justice required from the legislature for that extensive, fertile and prosperous country, between our northern line and the central canal, an improvement which would penetrate and pass through it about midway. I would advise the examination of this route by competent engineers, to ascertain its feasibility and its advantages. If upon full information this work should be determined upon and carried out, then, four grand lines of improvement passing from the western limits of the state eastward across the Blue Ridge, would pour the rich tides of that really fine country into the tide-water cities, and would unite, in one common and familiar brotherhood, the inhabitants of all "the grand divisions" of the state. In place of three divisions there would be no division, and instead of the senseless jealousy which now exists, one common interest, as one common parentage and glory, would unite them in a single effort for the advancement of the common happiness and prosperity of all.

Another connection between the tide-water of Virginia and the Ohio river, by means of a railroad, has been settled on in the public mind; nor will it be abandoned until the work is completed. Its importance, no one familiar with the results most likely to accrue from it will doubt. Its feasibility has been demonstrated by actual surveys, and the only question still in doubt of material moment to the project, is, at what point the Ohio river shall be reached.

In determining this, a proper regard must be had to the chartered rights already secured to other companies, and care be taken to prevent a rivalry between the works, which might endanger the complete success of either. This great object can be attained, in my opinion, by selecting Louisville in Kentucky as the western terminus for the road; and it is of no moment whether this road be a branch of the Virginia and Tennessee railroad, the Louisa road, or a branch of the Alexandria and Gordonsville road, crossing through Manassa's gap and passing thence westward to the proposed point. The route is accessible to each, and will, in my opinion, amply remunerate the patrons of each, although all of them should unite in the work, and depend for their profit upon the respective branches connecting with the main trunk, which would extend from Covington to Louisville. The construction of a railroad from tide-water to Louisville, upon this route, has been a favorite idea with me for many years, and I am sure is one which will challenge the approbation of all reflecting men, who will take the trouble to investigate the subject.

The surveys of competent engineers have shewn that Covington is of easy access from tide-water. From thence to Louisville, although no engineer has surveyed it, I venture the opinion, is a route of more easy accomplishment, than any other now proposed, lying between

the northern boundary of New York, and the valley of Tennessee.
The great barrier of the Alleghany is, upon this line, in the county of
Monroe, depressed into a gentle ascent, scarcely perceptible to a tra-
veller on horseback.   The insurmountable obstacle which the Cumberland mountains present every where else sinks down between Virginia and Kentucky, at the head-waters of the Sandy river in the
county of Tazewell, into a low and narrow ridge.   The residue of
the line to Lexington, Kentucky, lies along easy and accessible valleys
and plains.   From Covington to the Kentucky line is less than 150
miles, and the distance from thence to Lexington, is still shorter.   So
that, when the united efforts of Virginia and Kentucky shall have accomplished the construction of less than three hundred miles of railroad, the falls of Ohio and the falls of James river will be united by
railroad and canal, in bonds of eternal fellowship.

The advantages of a connection at Louisville are numerous and
very striking.   The navigation of the river below that point is seldom,
for any length of time, impeded by ice in winter or the drought of
summer and fall.   Not so above.   With this connection, the merchandize, intended for the winter and early spring supplies of a very large
portion of the West, would most certainly be distributed from Louisville, having reached there from the Northern cities by this unimpeded
southern route, whilst the water communication at the North would
have been closed, so to remain for months afterwards.   Nor is there
any railroad north of us which could compete successfully, with this
combined water line and railroad in the transportation of merchandize
or produce.   The diminished distance and the mild climate must
settle in our favor, beyond a doubt, the question of competition.   But
this link of railroad from Covington to Louisville is but a very short
one in the great chain, of which it will certainly form a part, stretch-
ing from the Atlantic ocean to the shores of the Pacific.   The energy
of the American people is aroused on the subject of this work, and its
accomplishment has already been determined upon in the public mind.
It cannot be believed that an improvement from which are to flow the
most momentous results, consequent upon any enterprize since the dis-
covery of the passage around the Cape of Good Hope, will be long
neglected by this great and prosperous nation.   The fruits of our
glorious war with Mexico will be imperfect—the monument which the
valour of our invincible armies has erected to our national grandeur
and renown, will be unfinished, without the construction of this most
stupendous work.

From the earliest history of the world down to this day, the commerce of India has been the prize for which the nations of the earth
have eagerly contended.   From the time when Hiram, King of Tyre,
sent his ships to bring gold from Ophir to decorate the temple of Solo-
mon, down to the last arrival of British merchantmen at the East India
docks in London, there has never failed a stream, bearing upon its
bosom spices and rich silks, jewels and pure gold, to give wealth, ele-
gance, refinement and power to the nation of people fortunate enough
to be its recipient.   Great cities have sprung up under its invigorating
influence, and won for themselves an immortal fame.   But, commerce

changing into a different channel, has left these once opulent marts a "desolation and reproach." The same consequences which have followed for thousands of years upon a given cause, cannot now fail in our day and country. By means of our possessions on the Pacific, the obstacle which this continent presents to the direct line of vessels from India to Europe, is not only removed, but made to afford means of a more rapid and safe intercourse than the ocean itself could secure.

If the East India commerce can then be brought across our continent upon a railroad, that road, seeking the best route, must pass through the midst of our commonwealth. From Norfolk, the best Atlantic seaport, or from any other tide-water city of Virginia, there is no difficulty in reaching the city of Louisville. At this point the Ohio can be easily bridged, affording, as it does, a rock foundation across the entire channel. From thence, through the states of Indiana and Illinois, the ground is favorable for a road, and the Mississippi itself furnishes a rock foundation for a bridge across its bosom, at "the Grand Tower," not far above the mouth of the Ohio. From this, if I am rightly informed, no water courses interpose barriers to the construction of a railroad, until the magnificent bay of San Francisco shall be reached. There is nothing, then, to hinder a car, laden with the rich silks and aromatic spices of India on the shores of the Pacific, from pursuing its continuous and uninterrupted course, until its journey is completed, and it rests upon the banks of the Chesapeake. To complete this line to the frontiers of the United States, Virginia, Kentucky, Indiana, Illinois and Missouri, are all equally interested. These five great central states are unequalled for fertility of soil and variety of product, mineral and agricultural. That their united efforts could achieve the completion of the work to our frontier, without materially feeling the burthen, is beyond cavil or dispute. This view is not chimerical. The object can be attained—the enterprize will be accomplished.

There is already a greater length of railroad in the United States, than would, if in a single line, connect the two great oceans—and the stock of all is profitable. But the combined commerce of all these roads is but a tithe of that which would pass across our continent from India—how then could the road fail to pay such profit as would amply compensate capital for its construction?

We cannot misunderstand or fail to appreciate the value of the prize; and the construction of the proposed road to Louisville, is a most powerful means of securing it to ourselves.

The legislature has been munificent towards the City of Alexandria, since its re-annexation to the commonwealth; and it is pleasing to know that this course is equally approved by the dictates of wisdom and of justice. This liberality has expedited the completion of that really great work, the Chesapeake and Ohio canal, as far as Cumberland, in the state of Maryland. Upon this canal, now nearly ready to be opened, presently will be transported a coal trade, inferior to none in America, either in the quantities carried down upon it, or in the quality of the mineral itself. Alexandria will be the chief mart for it, and the commerce, thereby brought to her wharves, will not only resuscitate her, but must give such impulse to all her interests, as cannot fail to raise the city to a high degree of prosperity and advancement. The works undertaken and proposed by her enterprising citizens, leading into the interior, are important to her wellbeing, as well as that of the country proposed to be reached by them. These works deserve the patronage and support of the commonwealth.

The other public works of the state are prosecuted generally, I believe, with energy, and promise much usefulness. The Danville railroad company is pushing on its work to completion with great vigor, and, as far as I have been able to ascertain, on the most favorable terms.

The subject of reform has engaged the attention of our citizens, more or less, ever since the adoption of our present heterogeneous and unwise constitution; it was the offspring of exaggerated sectional jealousy—not of an earnest desire to reform abuses too intolerable to be borne. The evident distrust of popular authority and control, which is written upon every page of it, has from its birth rendered it justly obnoxious to the people at large. It is most unfortunate that greater concessions were not made, then, to the exercise of power by the people—a few alterations in some particulars would, in all probability, have obviated the necessity of another convention for half a century, notwithstanding the inherent defects of the constitution. These defects render a call now inevitable, and certainly nothing short of a thorough constitutional reform will satisfy the demands of the people. The sooner this is accomplished, the better for all the interests of the commonwealth.

The county court system, as such, is repugnant to the fundamental principles of republican government—it has high judicial powers, it has high legislative authority—the power of taxation and of selecting and appointing important executive officers. It is a self-perpetuating body, responsible to no earthly power for its action, not even to the people whom they tax, and whose money they expend for any purpose whatever, that to them may seem good. The practical ill effects of the system have been less felt by the community, because of the generally highly intelligent and meritorious character of the magistrates themselves. As a body, the magistracy of Virginia is of the very highest respectability; but whilst it affords me real pleasure to bear testimony to this fact, I am constrained to say that the power confided to their hands, should be entrusted to officers directly responsible to the people.

But the most glaring wrong perpetrated upon the rights and intelligence of the people, is to be met with in those provisions touching the right of suffrage. The rule controlling that high privilege, now, is a purely arbitrary one. The principle governing the right of suffrage under the old constitution is discarded, because too restricted—and the *reason* for it, discarded also. It is a rule now, without principle, and without reason to support it; senseless and insulting in the distinctions which it draws, and most pernicious in the consequences which flow from it. The abrogation of this provision of the constitution, and the substitution of the proper one in its stead, would, in my opinion, well justify the expense and trouble consequent upon the call of a convention. The ground upon which the old constitution placed the right was distinct and definite. It went upon the idea, that the owners of the soil should not only govern that, but should govern every thing else beside. The absurdity of that idea has long been exploded; and it is now repudiated by the enlightened statesmen of every state in the Union.

The principle of universal suffrage ought to be adopted. Justice requires it, and the spirit of the age demands it at the hands of the commonwealth. Every free white man, a citizen of the state, over twenty-one years of age, should be allowed to vote in the county where he resides—but no where else. The right to vote in as many counties as can be reached by a man holding real or pretended title to land therein, is an insult to reason and an outrage upon popular rights: it is calculated to give to the cities and towns a control over the interests of the surrounding country, which can result in nothing but injury and discontent. This is one of the crying evils—a nuisance rendered sacred by constitutional enactment, which the public mind revolts at, and will have remedied.

The judiciary system needs reform; and I believe I am warranted in saying, such is the almost universal sentiment of our entire population. It is useless, however, for me to attempt a specification of the evils which need redress; they are quite familiar to all.

I earnestly recommend that a law be passed, requiring a poll to be opened in each county, to test the sense of the people, at the ensuing election, upon the call of a convention. If it results in a call, the succeeding legislature can settle the necessary preliminaries for its meeting, and, in the mean time, the census will be taken, so as to afford ample information to guide you in your deliberations.

You will, I am sure, be gratified to learn that the schools and colleges generally throughout the commonwealth are in an unprecedentedly flourishing condition. The University of Virginia, so long and so generously fostered by the commonwealth, is now giving most ample proof of the wisdom of the policy heretofore pursued towards it by your body. It is in a more prosperous condition now than at any previous previous period of its history, and bids fair to fulfil completely the objects had in view by its illustrious founder. The annual reports of the institution are herewith transmitted.

The Military Institute, commenced as an experiment by the state, has turned out most triumphantly successful, and is exhibiting capacities for usefulness certainly unsurpassed, and scarcely equalled, by any other system of education known amongst us. The spirit of reckless insubordination so common at other colleges, and by thoughtless young men often considered a grace rather than a reproach, at this institution is unknown. The military feature of the school works like a charm, and the point of honor with the student is subordination to the laws and obedience to discipline. Habits of regularity, system and order are acquired here, which must be of incalculable advantage throughout all after life to the graduate.

I think the public interest would be greatly advanced by an enlargement of the means of accommodation for students, and by the endowment of additional professorships; and I am persuaded that the appointment of a competent professor of agricultural chemistry in this institution, and in the University, would confer lasting and invaluable benefits upon the state at large. I herewith transmit to you a letter from Col. Smith, the able and efficient principal of the Military institute, relative to this professorship, and the propriety of establishing a farm in connection with the school. The suggestions are of the highest interest to the state, and deserve to be adopted.

I also invite your attention to the Medical College located in the City of Richmond. This institution was founded by individual enterprize, and has been almost wholly sustained by its professors. The general assembly granted it loans from the Literary fund, amounting to $25,000, to defray the expense of erecting the college edifice, but required interest upon these loans to be paid by the faculty. They have regularly complied with the requisition in good faith, although it has cost them, to do this, and to meet other necessities of the institution since its establishment, one half of their entire professional fees. By such efforts of its professors the institution has secured a firm place in the public confidence and respect, and reached a high degree of prosperity. The number of students is now larger than ever before, and there is good reason to anticipate continued and increasing success in the future.

The subject of medical education is of great economical interest to the state. It appears from document No. 37 of the last legislature that the aggregate expenditure abroad of Virginia students for this species of education, during the last forty years, has been some $3,000,000, exclusive of interest. From satisfactory sources of information, it has been ascertained that the number of medical students from this state, who attended lectures abroad during the last winter, was not less than 225, who carried with them and expended in other states at least $100,000. It is also a fact that two-sevenths of the matriculations from other states than Pennsylvania, in the two leading medical colleges of Philadelphia, last winter, were of students from this commonwealth. A liberal policy on your part towards a medical institution at home, combining as many advantages as the college in Richmond, would do much to check this disposition of our young men to go abroad at such an annual tax upon the resources of the state, and would result, as the liberal policy of the legislature towards the University of Virginia has resulted, in building up a flourishing institution at home, which will not only attract the great majority of Virginia students, but large numbers of young men from other states, to its halls.

To relieve the faculty of this institution from paying the interest now required of them, would relieve them of a burden which greatly depresses their energies and hangs heavily upon the prosperity of their college. I think the measure would advance the interests of medical science in Virginia, and be an act of justice and wise liberality towards the professors of that institution.   I recommend it therefore to your favorable consideration.

It affords me great pleasure to assure you of an improvement in the agricultural condition of the commonwealth generally.   The energy, industry and intellect of a large portion of our best citizens have been devoted with assiduity for some years past to this ennobling pursuit. The consequence of course is, not only a rapid advancement in the profits of the state at large from that source, but a very highly improved appearance in the face of the country itself.   It is worthy of remark, that whilst Virginia has extended, with great liberality, assistance to education and works of improvement, she has never given to agriculture any encouragement whatever.   This is the more surprising when we reflect that upon this great pursuit rest all the interests of society.   Let agriculture flourish and prosper, and no occupation of society will fail to thrive.   There have been at all times, too, in the legislature, a large number of members engaged in and identified with agriculture; but, up to this time, they have been content to labor for other interests, thought to be of more pressing importance, and to postpone, with a liberal disinterestedness, that which pertained more particularly to their own pursuits.   If there is in the commonwealth a pursuit which deserves encouragement from the legislature, undoubtedly it is agriculture.   If you take the planters, graziers and farmers of Virginia together, they constitute a body unsurpassed for all the qualities of intellect and character that adorn a people; and, if some means were adopted by the legislature to concentrate their efforts for the advancement of their occupation, a very little time only would be required to improve the agriculture of the state to its highest pitch.

A bill of the last session, providing for the appointment of an agricultural chemist for the state, was one of great merit, and calculated to promote the interest of the commonwealth.   I think its passage a matter of the first importance.

I would also recommend to the favorable consideration of the legislature, the propriety of appropriating annually such sums of money as may be necessary to sustain a properly organized state agricultural society.   This course has been pursued by several states of the North, and in every case with beneficial results.   The annual appropriations of New York for this purpose amount to about $8000; and, as far as I can learn, have given the greatest impetus to agricultural prosperity in all its branches.

You will perceive from the report of the superintendent of the penitentiary, that this institution continues to be prosperous and useful. The order and system, which characterize its management, ensure strict discipline, and as large a profit as can be realized from prison labor.   I concur fully in the suggestion of the superintendent touching the minimum term of imprisonment.   One year is wholly inadequate for any beneficial effect upon the prisoner; the term is too short to acquire any knowledge whatever of a trade, whilst the degradation and disgrace are as great as for the longest period of confinement.   The labor of the convict for so short a period will be wholly unproductive to the state, and the term of discipline too short for even a hope of reformation. The transportation of the offenders from the remote parts of the commonwealth, will be a serious item of additional expense. I am satisfied that the minimum period of punishment in the penitentiary should not be less than three years; it gives time to acquire some knowledge of a trade, whilst the discipline for that length of time will afford some hope of reformation. For crimes of less magnitude than those deserving this length of confinement, imprisonment in the county jail, and the infliction of corporal punishment, would seem to satisfy the ends of justice.

I also transmit to you a report of the adjutant-general, relative to the condition of the volunteer companies in the state. The views it embraces, I recommend to your particular attention.

Recent events in the campaigns of Mexico have demonstrated the utility and efficiency of this description of troops, even in an army of invasion. For purposes of defence at home, they would be scarcely, if at all, inferior to regular troops. Virginia possesses peculiar advantages, growing out of the system of education at her military institute, for rendering this arm of the militia perfectly effective. The encouragement of volunteer companies in the large towns and cities of the commonwealth, is most obviously proper, and to this end it is very desirable that the men should be exempted from service upon juries. The tax in time and money, necessarily imposed upon the members of volunteer companies, is very onerous; and, when augmented by the probable call to serve in the jury box, is rendered insupportable to men who depend upon their personal exertions for their livelihood. To relieve them from this duty would be a source of great encouragement to the volunteer system, and I therefore recommend it to the legislature.

A society has been organized by a number of gentlemen of talent and respectability, having for its object the collection and preservation of all the facts connected with the history of Virginia. The usefulness of such an association is evidently a matter of the greatest importance to the proper elucidation of our early history. It is to be feared that many valuable facts are irremediably lost through the neglect of this precaution. The warfare which won the territory of Virginia from the aborigines of the country was one of the most remarkable to be met with in the records of any country. Expeditions of the greatest danger, full of important consequences to the infant settlements, were frequently undertaken, prompted alone by individual prowess and enterprise. This desultory conflict, being perpetually waged, resulted finally in the conquest of our territory to the banks of the Ohio. In its progress many scenes of thrilling interest and startling adventure characterized the strife. These incidents will be regarded by future generations as essential muniments of our title to national glory and renown.

This society has already entitled itself to the gratitude of the state, from the publications it has made, connected with the early voyages to America. Virginia owes it to herself to give her legislative countenance and assistance to this meritorious undertaking.

The attention of the legislature has been earnestly called on several occasions to the subject of the free negro population in the commonwealth, but as yet no system has been adopted concerning the future disposition of them. I am strongly inclined to think that the most feasible plan, yet proposed for the reduction of their numbers, is to give ample assistance to the Colonization society. The best and wisest men of our nation have given it their countenance and support; and I cannot perceive that any practical improvement upon it has ever been suggested. It is a subject which demands your particular attention.

I herewith transmit to you resolutions of the Missouri legislature, touching the subject of federal interference with slavery. They are wise, temperate and patriotic, such as must command the respect and approbation of every Virginian.

I also transmit resolutions passed by the legislature of New Hampshire, of an opposite character, upon the same subject. It is painful to see principles and opinions, so disorganizing and ruinous in their tendencies as those embodied here, taking deep root in the minds and feelings of a people so richly deserving of our admiration in many particulars as those of New Hampshire.

This fearful question now agitating the country in its entire length is one fraught with the most momentous consequences, and is one upon which the destiny of the Union itself seems to hang. The " free soil" party claim for congress the right to exclude slavery from all the territories of the United States; and, acting upon this assumption, they declare their purpose of prohibiting the southern man from emigrating with his slaves to any of the national domain not now erected into a slave state.

It is difficult for those beyond the influence of the fanaticism which suggests and sustains these dangerous and disorganizing doctrines, to bring themselves to believe that such gross injustice and wrong could be seriously thought of by any deliberative body. The tendency of the movement is directly to disunion; the consummation of it will be the overthrow of our free institutions. If any great question of human liberty was involved in the issue; if any grand or striking system of policy, affecting the glory of the nation, depended upon its success; then there might be some reason found to excuse the jeopardy into which the country is plunged by it. But we look in vain for any justification of the sort. The movement originated in a wild fanaticism, and is persisted in from mere wantonness and lust of power. Not even the flimsy veil of a transcendental philanthropy for the negro slave is offered, to conceal the revolting features of the black treason against the constitution of the nation; for there would not be one slave the less in all America, even should congress append the " Wilmot Proviso" to every law upon the statute book. If this party were sincere in their desires to wipe out " the blot of slavery" from American soil, they should seek to introduce it into that portion of our country where the climate, soil and productions would all appeal with power to the master to liberate the slave.

Let the slave be carried where he is a burthen rather than a source of profit, and self-interest will prompt his liberation there, much more certainly than the zealous efforts of a disinterested piety in the regions where cotton and tobacco grow. But the tender consideration of the "free soiler" for the African, confines him forever in the country where it is profitable to keep him in perpetual bondage. It is very evident that, if the slaves of Virginia and Kentucky were distributed over all the country ceded to the United States by Virginia in 1787, the probabilities of their liberation would be increased many hundred fold, even without the appliances so freely but ineffectually resorted to now in various parts of the Union.

The terms of deep and bitter reproach which the fanatics of the North heap upon the South, as being disfigured with the "blot of African bondage"—a land withering under the "curse of slavery"—are not to be reconciled with a simple desire to exclude slavery from the territories, which is their avowed object. In spite of any disclaimer—in spite of a professed veneration for the sacred constitution we value so much, a determination to overthrow slavery is manifest in their course of procedure. They have either resolved to dissolve the Union, or, believing that the South has not the spirit to resist, have determined to invade the sanctuaries of our homes and liberate our slaves.

There might be discovered some justification in the course of outrage pursued towards us, if, upon a comparison, our country and people sank into insignificance by the side of our revilers. But bigotry itself would not venture such a charge. Our slave-holding country furnishes the staple products which foster foreign commerce, and secures to the North the wealth and prosperity they enjoy and boast of. The "curse" of slavery has not filled our land with felony and crime. We have no riots, mobs, arson and wholesale murder to mourn over, to punish or to countenance. We have no work-houses crowded with famishing and unprovided wretchedness; no swarms of beggars infesting our cities; no onerous poor rates levied to support everlasting pauperism. All is peace, quiet and order. From one extremity of the land to the other, there is felt, in every ramification of society, perfect and absolute personal security.

The intellectual culture of our country will scarcely be considered inferior to that of our non-slaveholding brethren at the North; whilst the patriotism and valour of our sons will certainly not suffer in comparison with any. Where and how this "blighting influence of slavery" manifests itself, it is impossible to see. Battling against the idea of slavery, they hazard the safety of the Union.

If a fanatical sentimentality is to break down the provisions of a written constitution, there is at once an end of the confederacy. It is worse than idle to discuss questions of ethics with the enthusiast, who denounces as "a curse" an institution established by the command of God himself, and who aspires to teach a morality purer than that of our Redeemer.

We plant ourselves upon the constitution itself, and rest our claims to protection upon its solemn guarantees. We desire no more power for slavery than is conferred by it; we ask no greater security. The querulous complaints which the fanatics make continually against the aggressive spirit of "the slave power," are calculated only to deceive their deluded followers. "The slave power" dictated the terms of the present Union, and gave up voluntarily that authority and control, which the agitators say it is now striving to lay hold on. The surrender of the Northwestern territory, under the ordinance of 1787, rendered it impossible that "the slave power" should ever after have the ascendancy in the Union. We ask for no superiority; but equality of rights, privileges and immunities, we not only ask for but are resolved to have.

There can be nothing more monstrous than the power claimed for congress to exclude slavery from the territories. Congress has no powers except those conferred on it by the express terms of the constitution, or such as are necessary to carry into effect those expressly granted. There is no clause in that instrument conferring upon congress authority to legislate upon the subject of slavery, in the territories or elsewhere; nor will it be pretended that the exercise of this power is necessary to carry into effect any expressly granted. To touch the subject at all, then, is a palpable and direct infraction of the constitution. The safeguards, which were thrown around the liberties of the people by the wisdom of those who framed the constitution, are demolished. Nothing is so simple as republican government, founded upon a written organic law, fixed and inflexible, to which all legislative action must conform. To this invention America owes its greatness and its liberty. -It is, however, in vain to talk of the supremacy of the people, idle to teach that they are the source of all power, unless the law which fixes the authority of the legislature shall be written and unchangeable. But allow the unauthorized action of the legislature to-day, to be given as a reason for the exercise of the same power to-morrow, and the rights of the people will be already usurped and their liberties in danger. Such, precisely, is the condition of things at this moment in the congress of the United States. The only shadow of justification they pretend to for the prohibition of slavery in the territories is, that the Missouri compromise, as it is termed, excluded it from all territory north of 36° 30′ of N. latitude. Without even a pretence of constitutional right for this action, they now urge it as a precedent giving authority to violate that compromise and to exclude slavery from all territory belonging to the United States. If we point to the letter of the constitution as the only source of authority, they point with triumph to the Missouri compromise. If we then insist upon the limits fixed by that agreement, they laugh at the credulity which attempts to define authority derived from precedent alone. Even now, by virtue of this single precedent, congress claims the power of abolishing slavery in the District of Columbia and in all the forts and arsenals belonging to the federal government in the South, as well as to prohibit the transportation and sale of slaves from one state to another. So we are not left to speculate upon the probable consequences of submitting to the unauthorized exercise of power in a given case. The fruits of it are plain; they are ruinous and never-ending aggressions.

The loyalty and devotion of Virginia to the Union are known to the world. They are written upon the enduring pages of our country's history. She was amongst the first to strike for constitutional liberty: she will be the last to abandon it. The great compromises upon which it rests she offered; and she herself suffered the chief sacrifices to secure its permanency—she has given with a liberality, which at this day can scarcely be reconciled with the dictates of wisdom. In all things touching the honor and glory of the confederacy, her hand has never been closed, except upon the sword.

She cannot submit to this usurpation of authority; this violation of her rights; this wanton degradation. Let us insist that the question be settled now and forever. Let us have no palliatives, no deceptive truces, no delays which only give strength to the spirit of aggression; no compromises which leave the question open for future adjustment. Let it be settled as to every foot of territory belonging to the United States, or which may hereafter be hers, by a compact as solemn and inviolable as the constitution itself. Any thing short of this is certain ruin to the South—it is annihilation. If a conflict must come, let it come now. We are strong in reality—stronger still in comparison with those whose hands are already raised against us. A few more years of acquiescence and supineness will bring about a necessity of an absolute submission to every wrong which oppression or contempt might heap upon our country.

Submission to the proposed action of congress is a virtual surrender of the entire South to the African race. If slavery is to be confined to its present limits, with a girdle of free states surrounding us, from the Atlantic to the Gulf of Mexico, a very few years, in a nation's history, will be sufficient to drive the white man beyond its limits. The sturdy laborer, the stay and support of every community, would soon leave the country swarming with negroes, for a residence in another land. The master, too, would presently follow, finding it impossible to remain. This view is no matter of conjecture merely; a simple rule of arithmetic will fix the fact and the time of its consummation, taking as a basis of the calculation the census of the last thirty years. Such are the fruits which the northern fanaticism, viewed in its most favorable aspect, must produce to the South. The consequences to the North will be little less disastrous. The great American staples must be cut short—the foreign commerce sustained by them will disappear from the seaports of our enterprising neighbours—their manufactures, should they be continued, must find a market abroad, in unprotected competition with the labor of Europe. The thrift and prosperity which now so pre-eminently characterize the working clases of New England and the North would vanish away; and the mechanic and laborer would discover, when too late, that, whilst striking the manacles of legal slavery from the hands of the African, he had riveted upon the necks of his own children the bondage of necessity, which no earthly power could ever again remove.

England's experiment with her West India colonies has proved a failure: this is admitted by all. It has not elevated the character of the negro man, nor has it contributed to his happiness. But the fatal consequences which are certainly to result to England from that stupendous folly, will, in the round of years, take from that colossal power the supremacy of the seas. It has struck a deadly blow at her colonial trade; and this was one of the chief elements of her maritime superiority. Shall examples of this sort teach us nothing? Is a blind fanaticism to overwhelm all things in its course?

This, I solemnly believe, is the most favorable view which can be taken of the subject, if Congress persists in its present course of aggression towards us.

But the wildest visionary would hardly expect to see these results brought peaceably about. Humanity itself must shudder at the bare contemplation of the slaughter most certainly to follow a prosecution of these iniquitous schemes. We cannot leave our homes: the ashes of Washington, Henry and Jefferson, may not be desecrated by the tread of the African's foot. The men of the South will not remain passive: the sword will not rest in the scabbard, whilst fanaticism is erecting at our hearth-stones an altar, upon which the victims of sacrifice are to be our daughters and our wives.

The almost unanimous sentiment of the slaveholding country upon this subject is not the result of political agitation seeking for party ascendancy. It is the spontaneous outburst of a whole people, upon the conviction that their dearest rights are menaced. Party prejudices and animosities are buried; every tenet of faith, and shade of political opinion, agree perfectly; and the novel spectacle is presented of eight millions of people, actuated by and obedient to a single determination, arising as one man to stay the hand of usurpation and wrong.

Let us trust that our brethren at the North will understand, before it is forever too late, that a feeling of self preservation, and not one of silly bravado, actuates our course. Let us hope still that our common sufferings and common triumphs, the memories of the past and the bright hopes of the future which we offer to all mankind, may stay the madness which is precipitating us into a ruin from which no human power can ever grant us even the hope of rescue.

JOHN B. FLOYD.

December 3, 1849.

VOLUNTEER COMPANIES.

To His Excellency Gov. FLOYD.

SIR,

In reply to your enquiries as to the importance of sustaining the volunteer corps of the state, and the most effectual means of attaining that object, I respectfully report, that the militia of the line in time of peace cannot, under any practicable system, be so trained and disciplined as to enable it to meet a sudden emergency.

The reliance of the state then, for the suppression of tumults, insurrections or other disturbances of the public peace or safety, or for repelling invasion, is, necessarily, upon the volunteer corps.

That public spirit which carries young men into their ranks, at an expense in time and money which many of them cannot well afford—their promptitude and efficiency upon every call, no matter on what occasion, eminently entitle the volunteers to the confidence and gratitude of the state, and to all the support and encouragement the legislature can give them.

Upon all occasions, in past time, they have instantly responded to every call upon them for *any* service. The insurrection of Southampton in 1831 affords a striking illustration of that fact. Intelligence of this occurrence reached the then governor, by express, at an early hour of the morning, and it was represented to be far more formidable and extensive than ultimately it proved to be. There was then but a single armed company between the seat of government and Southampton, and not one stand of public arms in that or any of the adjacent counties. An instant call upon the volunteers threw into Southampton, within twenty-four hours after the governor received intelligence, a force sufficient to have put down any number of insurgents that could have been embodied. The dawn of the next morning after the issuing of the governor's orders, found the Richmond artillery with a complete field train, and 1000 stand of arms for the militia, upon the ground, and in a few hours more, the Richmond troop of cavalry and a battalion of volunteers from Norfolk and Portsmouth.

But for these volunteers, it is undeniable that no militia force, sufficient to meet the emergency, could have been embodied and armed in several days. What has happened may happen again, and in that case there can be no doubt that, without an efficient force of volunteers, the consequences would be serious. ˙ It is therefore absolutely necessary to meet the question, how such a force can most certainly be kept up. Experience has proved that the provisions of law heretofore designed for that object are insufficient—for in every quarter the volunteer corps are few in number, and can with difficulty be sustained.

Among the encouragements (so called,) now held out to them, is the exemption from ordinary militia duty after seven successive years' service—but that is not sufficient. The new law allows each armed and uniformed company to enrol not more than 50 contributing members, who are to be exempt from duty on paying $3 each per annum. But this will amount to nothing—for who will pay $3 for exemption in a volunteer company, when he may get it by remaining in the line for $1 50?

The volunteers want some provision of law which will *fill up their ranks*—which 50 or even 100 contributing members would not do, even if they could be obtained.

These corps are almost entirely composed of young men just entering upon, or in the prime of manhood, who are either engaged in business for themselves or in the employment of others. In the cities and towns, the latter is most generally the case. But in either, the time required for volunteer service cannot always be spared. If, however, the exemption which the law allows to members of fire companies were extended to the volunteers—it would have the effect, certainly in the cities and towns, and, probably, generally, of filling their ranks. Take, for example, the city of Richmond, where there are no less than five jury courts, one or more almost always sitting, and, consequently requiring a large number of jurymen. Any man will prefer to give his own services or the services of those in his employment to a volunteer company, to being himself or to having them subject to be called upon at any time to serve as jurors for days and sometimes for weeks, when perhaps his own private business is of the most pressing character.

Exemption, then, from jury duty is the most efficient encouragement that the law can give; and, apart from the intrinsic importance of having a well organized volunteer force to meet any emergency, it would be but a moderate equivalent for services, as disinterested and patriotic as any can be.

I have the honor to be,

Very respectfully,

Your obed't. serv't.

WM. H. RICHARDSON,
Adj't. Gen'l.

AGRICULTURAL PROFESSORSHIP.

VIRGINIA MILITARY INSTITUTE,
Nov. 24, 1849.

Gen. WM. H. RICHARDSON,
                    Adjutant-General.

DEAR SIR,

I am in receipt of your favour of the 19th instant, making enquiries relative to the suggestion of the governor, recommending an agricultural professorship for this institution. I consider the suggestion a most valuable one, and I am glad that I have the *data* at hand to shew its entire practicability. These *data* are derived from the detailed reports of our subsistence department, by which I am enabled to give you more precise information on the points referred to in your letter, than can probably be derived from any other quarter.

Should the recommendation of the governor be carried out, and a farm purchased for the experimental operations of the agricultural professorship, the subsistence department of the institute would furnish a home demand for its surplus products; and if properly conducted, it might readily supply all the agricultural products now consumed by a corps of 120 cadets. This consumption embraces the following articles:

Milk, 20 galls. per day, at 12½ cts.,			2 50	
Butter, 30 lbs. do. 12½ cts.,			3 75	
Vegetables do.	-	-	2 00	
Fruits, - do.	-	-	2 00	
			——3,600 per annum.	
Flour, 150 bbls. at $ 4,	-	-	600	"
Corn, 450 do. at 50 cts.	-	-	225	"
Pork, 10,000 lbs. at $ 4,	-	-	400	"
Beef, 20,000 lbs. at $ 5,	-	-	1000	"
Poultry, (estimated,)	-	-	200	"
Total annual consumption,	-		$ 6025	"

I would not expect the farm at first to furnish the supplies at lower rates than we are now paying, but it might reasonably be expected that when science and art had been judiciously applied to its cultivation as a *model* farm, one half the number of cattle now required would supply the milk and butter, and the increasing productiveness of the land would diminish the expense of all the agricultural products.

So much for the economy of the governor's recommendation.

But the suggestion claims great consideration, when viewed as a scheme for organizing a *school of agriculture*. The professor, being placed in charge of the operations of the farm, would be expected not only to give his classes the most minute instruction in experimental farming, but, keeping constantly in view that the characteristic feature of the institute is to give its graduates practical and business qualifications and habits, he would arrange a system of tables and journals, shewing the daily operations of each part of the farm, including a record of observations, &c. In these duties, he should be assisted by regular details of his class, while the period of encampment might be most profitably employed in a more extended acquaintance with the out-door operations of the farm, and with occasional geological explorations. You can well imagine what results might thus be obtained in an institution organized and conducted as this is upon strictly military principles—and the state would soon appreciate the importance of the information which the monthly reports of this department would afford to its agriculturists. As a specimen of the practical information to be derived from daily records of operations, the accompanying monthly statement of our mess-hall consumption, upon which the estimates in the first part of this letter are based, need only be carefully examined. I need not advert to the importance of such a *model farm* in supplying the state with the most approved species of seed, roots, fruit, &c. while its central position would afford facilities to farmers to witness its operation.

In connection with these views, I might call your attention to the fact, that our board of visitors, at their annual meeting in July, under a conviction that the chair of physical sciences in this institution was overcharged with duties, have urged the establishment of a new professorship. The views of the governor might, therefore, be most advantageously tried, by placing, for the present, the agricultural professor in charge of the department of chemistry. By giving him the aid of a principal assistant in chemistry, the duties above enumerated might very well be associated with instruction in chemistry.

It would of course be expected that the agricultural professor should keep a strict account of profit and loss upon all species of cultivation tried, with all of which practical instruction should be given to his class.

> I am, very respectfully,
>
> Your obed't serv't,
>
> FRANCIS H. SMITH.

P. S. I might add, that great economy would result to us in having the washing of the cadets done at the farm. This might be advantageously effected by employing the heat used in boiling the roots, &c. for cattle, for the washing apparatus. We pay now $1800 a year for washing.

RESOLUTIONS

ON THE

SUBJECT OF SLAVERY.

STATE OF MISSOURI.

Resolved by the general assembly of the state of Missouri:

1st. That the federal constitution was the result of a compromise between the conflicting interests of the states which formed it; and in no part of that instrument is to be found any delegation of power to congress to legislate on the subject of slavery, excepting some special provisions having in view the prospective abolition of the African slave trade, and for the recovery of fugitive slaves; any attempt therefore, on the part of congress, to legislate on the subject, so as to affect the institution of slavery in the states, in the District of Columbia, or in the territories, is, to say the least, a violation of the principle upon which that instrument was founded.

2nd. That the territories acquired by the blood and treasure of the whole nation, ought to be governed for the common benefit of the people of all the states; and any organization of the territorial governments, excluding the citizens of any part of the Union from removing to such territories with their property, would be an exercise of power by congress, inconsistent with the spirit upon which our federal compact was based; insulting to the sovereignty and dignity of the states thus affected; calculated to alienate one portion of the Union from another, and tending ultimately to disunion.

3d. That this general assembly regard the conduct of the Northern states, on the subject of slavery, as releasing the slaveholding states from all further adherence to the basis of compromise fixed on by the act of congress of the 6th of March 1820, even if such act ever did impose any obligation upon the slaveholding states, and authorizes them to insist upon their rights under the constitution; but for the sake of harmony, and for the preservation of our federal Union, they will still sanction the application of the principles of the "Missouri compromise" to the recent territorial acquisitions, if by such concession future aggressions upon the equal rights of the states may be arrested and the spirit of anti-slavery fanaticism be extinguished.

4th. The right to prohibit slavery in any territory belongs exclusively to the people thereof, and can only be exercised by them in forming their constitution for a state government, or in their sovereign capacity as an independent state.

5th. That in the event of the passage of any act of congress, conflicting with the principles herein expressed, Missouri will be found in hearty co-operation with the slaveholding states, in such measures as may be deemed necessary for our mutual protection against the encroachments of Northern fanaticism.

6th. That our senators in congress be instructed, and our reprentatives be requested to act in conformity to the foregoing resolutions.

Resolved by the house of representatives, the senate concurring therein, That the secretary of state be required to transmit a copy of the resolutions passed at this session of the general assembly on the subject of slavery, to the executive of each of the states of the Union, with the request that the same be laid before their respective legislatures, and also a copy to each of our senators and representatives in congress.

Approved March 10, 1849.

STATE OF NEW HAMPSHIRE.

The select committee, to whom were referred the report and resolutions of the legislature of Virginia, and also certain resolutions of the legislature of Missouri, upon the subject of fugitive slaves and other matters pertaining to the institution of slavery, respectfully

REPORT:

That without entering into any general examination of the reasoning of the report in question, your committee are of opinion that many of the topics therein discussed are such as to require no action on the part of New Hampshire. This state has "commenced" no "war of legislation against the owners of fugitive slaves." It has assumed no position upon which it may not rightly stand, without violation of the principles, either of justice, humanity or the constitution. It has been actuated by no "feigned philanthropy;" neither "irresponsible mobs, composed of fanatics, ruffians, and fugitive slaves," nor mobs in any other way constituted, have had any recent existence here. That "irregular outbreaks of brutal violence and ferocity have happened in the free states," that "insane fanatics and brutal ruffians" have in these scenes been continually violating the rights of those who own slaves, is asserted in the report under consideration, in language far too broad for truth, and far too angry for that courtesy which ought to be observed in the intercourse between sovereign states. That these pictures are drawn with more feeling than fidelity, and are the result of a distempered fancy rather than an impartial observation of facts, our knowledge of the orderly and law-observing character of non-slaveholding communities compel us to believe.

We trust that the report in question does a similar injustice to the slaveholding communities for which it speaks, when it intimates that if the laws are not modified and executed to their satisfaction, they will invade the territory of the free states, and re-act upon their Southern frontiers, forays which occurred upon the borders of Scotland in a semi-barbarous age!

We should regret the occurrence of such scenes. We should regret the attempt, threatened in various alternatives and in various parts of the report in question, to divide this Union, or excite an armed resistance to its laws. But yet we most confidently believe that our institutions are inherent with power sufficient for their own protection, and that of every portion of the American people.

The new legal remedy asked for by the report under consideration is indeed remarkable. That every postmaster and collector in the free states shall be clothed with the same judicial power over the rights and liberty of persons claimed as slaves, as courts of the United States may now exercise—that every member of this newly constituted host of magistrates, may surround himself with marshals, possessing every summary process—that all improper acts, occurring whenever and wherever, in presence of any considerable number of persons, an alleged fugitive slave is demanded or held in custody, shall be removed from the jurisdiction of the state courts to the courts of the United States—are claims so extraordinary, so insulting to the free states, that they cannot have been advanced with any expectation of their meeting with the sanction of any state where a regard to the interests of slavery has not become paramount to every proper appreciation of state rights, and of the rights and security of freemen.

The report of the Virginia legislature complains that the New England states, with a sterile soil and ungenial climate, have become, in proportion to their population, the most wealthy communities in the world, while comparative poverty has fallen upon the South, and its commerce and navigation have been transferred from its own harbors to those of the North. It might have drawn a like comparison between Ohio and Kentucky—between free territory and slave territory at every point where they come in contact. Is it strange that the free states, with these facts every where spread out before them, should be unwilling to see slavery extended, with its blighting influences, over territories now free?

The committee conclude this report by recommending the adoption of the following resolutions:

1. *Resolved by the senate and house of representatives, in general court convened,* That, opposed to every form of oppression, the people of New Hampshire have ever viewed with deep regret the existence of slavery in this Union; that while they have steadfastly supported all sections in their constitutional rights, they have not only lamented its existence as a great social evil, but regarded it as fraught with danger to the peace and welfare of the nation.

2. *Resolved*, That while, in periods of excitement, the opponents of slavery have resorted to measures which we have thought it our duty to oppose and censure, on the other hand slaveholding communities, in many portions of this confederacy, have engaged in excitements and resorted to measures equally deserving the severest condemnation.

3. *Resolved*, That we stand pledged by our course from the adoption of the federal constitution to the present time, to respect all the rights which that instrument guarantees to the slave states. .

4. *Resolved*, That while we respect the rights of the slaveholding as well as the free portions of this Union—while we will not willingly consent that wrong be done to any member of the glorious confederacy to which we belong, we are firmly and unalterably opposed to the extension of slavery over any portion of American soil now free.

5. *Resolved*, That the American Union is strongly based upon the affections of an overwhelming majority of the American people—that we trust that it will outlive for ages the threats with which fanaticism assails it—that in its hour of peril, stout hearts and strong arms will be ready in every corner of our land to defend it—and that it will long continue here a proud ark of freedom, firm and enduring, the time-tried model after which shall be fashioned those free institutions which are hereafter to bestow their incalculable blessings upon the whole world.

6. *Resolved*, That in our opinion congress has the constitutional power to abolish the slave trade and slavery in the District of Columbia, and that our senators be instructed and our representatives requested to take all constitutional measures to accomplish these objects.

7. *Resolved*, That his excellency the governor be requested to transmit copies of the foregoing report and resolutions to the governors of the several states of the Union, and also a copy of the same to each of the senators and representatives of this state in the congress of the United States.

SAMUEL H. AYER,
Speaker of the House of Representatives.

WILLIAM P. WEEKS,
President of the Senate.

Approved, July 7, 1849.

SAMUEL DINSMOOR, *Governor.*

Document 2

MESSAGE

Gentlemen of the Senate and House of Delegates :

The peace and prosperity which have been vouchsafed to the people of our commonwealth, is a subject of sincere congratulation, and is cause of thanksgiving to the Almighty Disposer of events.

At the time of your adjournment, serious apprehensions were felt in regard to the near approach of the pestilence which was raging in other lands. It has visited our cities, and whilst we have to mourn the loss of some of our valuable citizens, it is a subject of thankfulness that its ravages have been light in comparison with the number of its victims during its previous visits. Since that time, too, our hearts have been saddened by the tidings that one of your own number has passed away from earth.

All the agencies of the state, provided for the enforcement of the laws, have been in successful operation, and there has been no serious disturbance of the public peace.

The exigencies of the situation, in which we find ourselves, will demand your mature and wise consideration.

The details of the financial operations of the state government for the last year, are contained in the report of the auditor of public accounts herewith transmitted, and your attention is invited to the recommendations therein contained. The report of the treasurer is also submitted.

Assuming the income of the last year as the basis for the estimate of this, there will be received into the public treasury during the year ending on the 30th September, 1867,   1,228,679 30

Add to this the amount on hand 1st October, 1866,   334,607 56
                                                                                     ─────────────
                                                                                     1,563,286 86

I estimate the expenses for carrrying on the government up to the 1st October, 1867, at - 510,000 08

Leaving a balance in the treasury of - - $1,053,286 86

In this estimate I have made a liberal allowance for the current
expenses of the government; for an appropriation to supply artificial
limbs to disabled soldiers; to pay the balance due on the statues for
the Washington monument; for the necessary appropriations to the
lunatic and deaf and dumb and blind asylums; for the penitentiary
and public guard, and for a geological survey. This estimate is made
on the supposition that a change will be made in the mode of defray-
ing criminal expenses. I am aware that a large number of petitions
for appropriations will be presented to the general assembly, all of
which will be urgently pressed by their advocates. But, in my esti-
mation, none of them have any merit to compare with the demand
on the state for the payment of the interest on the public debt. I
should fail in my duty, did I not urge upon you the paramount obligation which rests upon us to make provision for the payment of this
interest in preference to any other claims, except those above indicated.

The public debt, with the interest funded, will
amount on the first day of January next, to - 43,383,679 27
Deduct amount owed by Sinking and Literary funds, 2,377,681 60

Balance for which interest is to be paid, - $41,005,997 67

This will require an additional assessment on property, real and
personal, of about 46 cents on the $100; which, added to the 14
cents on the $100 now assessed, will make 60 cents on the $100 required to pay the expenses of the government, necessary appropriations and interest on the public debt. In this calculation no estimate
is made of the expenses of the collection of the additional tax of
about $1,500,000. If the change in the mode of collection pro-
posed in my last annual message, shall be made, no additional expense will be incurred.

It is thought by some, that the people are not able to pay the tax
required for the payment of the whole interest on the public debt
this year. You are fresh from the people, and of this ought to be

the best judges. There has been some vague talk about repudiating
or scaling the public debt. This I am satisfied proceeds from
want of consideration. To say nothing of the morality of the act,
no step would be so prejudicial to all our future interests as a
serious discussion of the subject. To commit the deed, would be to
cut off all private credit from without the state, and erect a bar to
the future influx of capital. If so fatal a step should be taken, no
gentleman would hereafter be particularly anxious, when abroad, to
be recognized as a Virginian.

The state has recovered slowly from the disasters of the late war.
The almost entire failure of the wheat crop last year, and the partial
failure this year, have greatly affected the amount of money in the
state. Under more favorable auspices, we hope next year for a better harvest: this will strengthen the public feeling, and drive all
idea of repudiation from the state. There is a disposition to postpone any payment of interest on the public debt, until it shall be
ascertained what portion of it is to be paid by West Virginia. I do
not think this would be good policy. About one-fifth of the taxable
property of the old state is contained in West Virginia. By the
terms of the division, West Virginia is to pay her equitable share of
the public debt. What proportion that will be, I am not prepared
to say. Commissioners on the part of this state, to confer, and settle
with like commissioners appointed by West Virginia, were chosen
near the close of your last session. This was about the time that
the legislature of West Virginia adjourned. They appointed no
commissioners. That legislature will not assemble until the middle of January: then commissioners will be appointed. It is not
likely that any settlement will be made before your adjournment.
If no provision shall be made for the payment of the interest on the
public debt until the commissioners shall have settled this question,
it will still further depreciate the bonds, and the interest will accu-
mulate—thus making it more difficult each succeeding year to resume
payment. If a time shall be fixed at which interest will be paid, in
whole or in part, it will at once appreciate the value of the bonds,
and thus greatly add to the available means of such of our own
people as hold them.

Various modes of paying this interest have been proposed. One is,
to pay two per cent. on the 1st January, 1868, and increase one per
cent. each succeeding year until six per cent. shall be attained; then

to fund the unpaid interest, to be paid at a future day; to issue new coupon bonds in accordance with the above plan, payable in twenty and forty years, at the option of the state, and to create at the same time a sinking fund looking to the redemption of the principal when it shall become due. If this plan shall be adopted, the proceeds of dividends from the railroads, the income derived from the oyster tax, and one per cent. of the annual taxes, might be made a sinking fund. I make the suggestion for your consideration.

I attach no value for revenue purposes to the stock held by the state in the James river canal, turnpikes and bridges, and in railroads commenced but not completed. The state owns about fifteen millions of dollars in stocks and bonds of railroads in active operation. These roads, by prudent management, ought to yield dividends in a few years sufficient to pay the interest on that amount of the public debt. I have no doubt that, if the general assembly will authorize it, in the course of two or three years, the stock and bonds held by the state in these roads can be exchanged for their full amount in the stock and bonds of the state, and I unhesitatingly recommend the passage of a law authorizing their sale. The act should authorize the sale of the stock and bonds of the Virginia and Tennessee, Southside and Norfolk and Petersburg roads together; and of the Richmond and Danville and the York river roads together. The Orange and Alexandria and the Virginia Central roads might be sold separately. All these roads, under the management of private companies, would soon yield handsome dividends and make the investment profitable.

The tobacco warehouse in the city of Richmond known as "Public warehouse," was partially burned in 1865, and has not been repaired. It ought to be sold—it will bring its fair value. I would recommend the appointment of three commissioners in this city to fix upon it a fair valuation, so that you may fix a minimum price for which it may be sold, with as much more as competition will bring. I think the same course should be pursued in regard to the old armory grounds.

An act was passed last winter, authorizing the Board of public works to sell certain unappropriated lands on the Chesapeake bay and on the seaboard. The lands are variously estimated to be worth from $50,000 to $100,000. It was found to be necessary to have those lands surveyed before they could be sold. The Board proceeded to organize a surveying corps, and I undertook to defray the expenses of the survey out of the contingent fund, and found it to be a work of much greater magnitude than was expected. The surveys were made at a cost of upwards of $3,000. Maps and plats of the land were carefully made. The Board intended to make sale of the lands, but claims were set up to some portions of them which clouded the titles. It is not believed that these claims are valid, but the Board had not time to investigate them, and thought it best to postpone the sales until they could be assured of the character of the claims set up, in order that the best prices might be secured.

Selden, Withers & Company.

In accordance with the act passed at your last session in regard to the claim of the state against Selden, Withers & Company, I employed counsel who is giving energetic attention to the subject, at Alexandria, Washington and St. Louis. After the conveyance made to the state by Mr. Withers, he made other conveyances and a will, and has since died. By these transactions the most of the property conveyed has become the subject of new difficulties. It is believed that from $75,000 to $100,000 will be eventually realized by the state from this debt, which was originally, I believe, nearly $500,000.

Norfolk and Petersburg Railroad Bonds.

In 1858, the general assembly authorized the Board of public works to subscribe on the part of the commonwealth, three hundred thousand dollars, in six per cent. state stock, to the Norfolk and Petersburg railroad, to enable the company to complete and equip their road; and provided that said company should deliver to the Board of public works a like amount of their first mortgage bonds in exchange for said stock. About the time of the evacuation of Richmond, in the spring of 1865, these bonds were stolen from the second auditor's office, where they had been deposited for safe keeping. I was informed, last winter, that a large amount of these bonds had found their way to Cincinnati, and would be delivered to the state for about five per cent. of their value. Upon consultation with the committee on finance, which was then in session, it was deemed best to take these bonds upon the terms offered, and pay the expense out of the contingent fund. I found that the bonds were in the hands of persons of doubtful character, and after much trouble succeeded in obtaining upwards of $100,000 of them. Parties seemed to be gathering them up in different sections of the country. A few were returned without charge. I found that it would cost the state a considerable amount of money to redeem them, as some parties, representing themselves as purchasers, asked to be paid fifty cents in the dollar. I therefore decided to purchase no more of them. We have now $113,000 of these bonds. In the spring of 1865, on discovering the loss of the bonds, notice was given to the Norfolk and Petersburg railroad company, and they were notified not to pay them. The public were also cautioned against purchasing them, through the newspapers. Although it is the law, I believe, in this country and in England, that coupon bonds, or coupons taken from a bond, pass on delivery, I think these bonds are not subject to this general law. A coupon bond, issued by a corporation, is peculiarly the creature of the legislature, and the corporation derives its power to make and sell from the act of assembly. The purchaser of a coupon bond can only be safe by knowing that the bond has been put upon the market in accordance with law. These bonds were authorized to be issued by the Norfolk and Petersburg railroad company, "to be delivered to the Board of public works," for the benefit of the state of Virginia. The Board of public works were only authorized to hold them for the benefit of the state; they were not authorized to sell, nor was authority ever given to any person to dispose of them. The authority to sell a coupon bond by a corporation, is as essential as the authority to make, to render it valid.

Oyster Laws.

The experience of the last year has shown that a handsome revenue can be derived from the tax on taking and carrying oysters. I would recommend that the two acts passed last winter on this subject, be reduced to one, and be amended so as to rid the law of all ambiguity. I can see no necessity for requiring every person who takes out a license to take oysters, to give bond and security. It makes the law too cumbersome. It costs, under the existing law, two dollars and forty cents to get three dollars and sixty cents into the treasury from those who take oysters. This is unreasonable, as there is no labor required from those engaged in collecting the tax adequate to the compensation paid. A question has been raised as to the constitutionality of the law; but no objection can be urged against it that could not be applied with equal force to any tax imposed by the state. There is no state in the world, that I know of, that does not claim and enforce the right to regulate the taking of game and fish within its borders. All experience has proven that it is eminently proper to protect oysters by regulating the time and mode of taking them, so as to prevent the diminution of their increase. The right to tax the taking and carrying of oysters is equally extensive with the right to protect them. It is claimed that to tax the taking, and then the carrying, of oysters is a double tax, and therefore illegal. This proposition is equally untenable, for the object of the law is to divide the tax between those who take and those who carry. It is further asserted that the law operates harshly on owners of large vessels engaged in carrying miscellaneous articles. All revenue laws will be found to operate harshly on some persons, and if these vessels are exempted, you may as well abandon the law; for they will carry all the oysters, and the small vessels engaged in the trade will be stopped. By perseverance and proper legislation, the oyster tax will be made to yield an annual revenue of more than two hundred thousand dollars.

Collection of Taxes.

I desire to renew the suggestions presented in my last annual message, in regard to the mode of collecting taxes. In considering the subject, you may prefer to leave the collection of the taxes with the sheriffs, requiring the collections to be made in the manner I have proposed. This will save to the people at least one hundred thousand dollars annually in the amount of their taxes.

Militia.

I herewith transmit the report of the adjutant general for the present year, from which it will be seen that there are one hundred and thirty-six regiments of militia of the line, of which number one hundred and seven have been organized. The remaining twenty-nine regiments are in process of organization. I refer you to the report for full details.

Penitentiary.

It will be seen by the report of the directors of the penitentiary,

that this institution has been self-sustaining, and has a balance to
its credit of nearly five hundred dollars. This is very creditable,
especially when we consider the large influx of convicts unacquainted
with mechanic arts. But a favorable opportunity presented itself of
employing a number of the colored convicts on the excavation of two
short railroad tracks, where they were employed, with mutual profit
to the institution and the contractor, and doubtless to the welfare of
the prisoners: they were not over-worked, and had the benefit of the
open air. I think it would be well to enlarge the authority of the
superintendent, with the sanction of the executive, to employ this
class of convicts outside of the penitentiary.

I urged the dispensing with the office of penitentiary storekeeper
last year, but the legislature differed with me. In conversing with
those long acquainted with the operations of the institution, I learn
that it has been the custom for the superintendent to sell large
amounts of work at the prison. These sales are for cash; the property is taken away, the money is paid to the superintendent, he pays
it over to the penitentiary storekeeper, and for counting and receiving the money the storekeeper gets the same per cent. as if the goods
had been taken to his store and there sold. There is no reason for
this, and a per centage ought not to be allowed on money going into
his hands in this way. He should only be allowed for the goods
placed in his store and by him sold. It is wrong to pay out money
to any officer where there is no compensation in service.

I am informed by the superintendent of the penitentiary, that for
the present, the out-door employment for colored convicts has ceased.
These, with the new convicts, have so swelled the number, that he has
now nearly one hundred prisoners more than he can employ in the
penitentiary. Additional buildings must be erected, or a new penitentiary built, unless means can be devised for the out-door employment of the convicts. I submit the whole subject for your
mature consideration.

"Criminal Charges."

Our "criminal charges" are becoming alarming, and the subject
calls for your serious consideration. The transportation of criminals
to the penitentiary is a heavy charge; ten cents a mile for the criminal, and the same for the sheriff and guard coming and returning, is

allowed by law. This is intended to pay expenses of sheriff and guard, one or two days' hotel bills in the city, and a per diem besides. The public guard is larger than is necessary to guard the penitentiary. A portion of this guard should be employed to bring the convicts to the penitentiary. Make it the duty of the clerk of each circuit court, as soon as the criminal trials of the term are concluded, to notify the superintendent of the penitentiary of the number of convicts to be sent from his county. A sufficient guard could then be sent to the county at once to bring the convicts. Under the circumstances, the officers of the railroads would cheerfully transport the guards and prisoners free of charge. I have maturely considered this subject, and am satisfied that seventy-five per cent of the cost on the present system, amounting to thousands of dollars, can be saved in this way, and all the ends of justice be as well, if not better served. As another mode of diminishing criminal charges, it is proposed that each county and corporation shall defray the expenses of its commonwealth's attorney, sheriffs, clerks, grand and petit juries, witnesses, jail fees, &c. I am satisfied that it will diminish the amount of tax on the people. There is no reason why the money should be collected and sent to the state treasury, and then paid back to the counties and corporations. But there are certain abuses in regard to these criminal charges that I have no doubt would be corrected; there is a prevalent opinion, that as the money comes out of the state treasury it may be spent more freely, and to say the least of it, great liberality is in many instances practiced. My object is to bring all these expenses as near to the tax payer as possible, and as he makes the officers, and pays the expenses, it will tend to produce at least circumspection. It will have a good tendency to keep the idea close to the tax payer that his taxes depend, to a certain extent, on the good order of the community: each man becomes to a greater extent a conservator of the peace. There is also a positive justice in this arrangement. In some counties there are but few persons, if any, in the jails, whilst in others the jails are crowded. There is no justice in taxing the counties where peace and order prevail, to assist more disorderly communities. Nor is it believed that the officers of the law would be any the less vigilant in bringing crime to punishment if the change were made.

The criminal charges in the cities are greatly augmented for want of some kind of workhouse, or mode of employing those convicted of petty offences. It has been credibly stated, that the boarding of the prisoners in the Richmond city jail costs more than the board of all the convicts in the penitentiary. This needs correction, and the law should be so altered as to reduce these expenses. I am inclined to think convicts in the jails in the country could be worked to some profit on the county roads—it would depend somewhat upon their number and the amount of guard necessary. I make the suggestions for your consideration. I believe that, by judicious legislation, you can reduce these suggestions to practice, save the people from a large amount of taxes for criminal expenses, and at the same time have better order.

In connection with this subject, I would respectfully recommend the abolition of the called courts. The reason for their existence has long since ceased. I think it will be found, on investigation, that the expenses of the called courts are equal to those of the final trial. The law should be so altered as to vest in the committing justice all the powers now exercised by the called court. I believe this is the only state in the Union where such a court has an existence.

I would recommend, too, that the county courts should have authority to try, at their monthly terms, persons charged with petit larceny, either by jury or by the court, at the election of the prisoner. Owing to the large amount of petit offences committed, and the inability of the persons charged, to give bail, this would greatly facilitate the administration of justice.

The Vagrant Law.

I would recommend modifications of the vagrant law passed last winter. The agents of the freedmen's bureau have called my attention to the fact that large numbers of freedmen are congregated in certain counties, some of whom are fit subjects for the poorhouse, admission to which has been refused them on the ground that they have no legal settlement in the county. The support of this class has been thrown upon the bureau, and objection is made, by the officers of the counties where they lived while slaves, when an attempt is made to send them back to their former places of abode. I hope you will devote such attention to the subject as it requires at your hands.

Registration of Freedmen.

I recommended to you, at your last session, the propriety of providing by law for a registry, to be kept by the clerk of each county court in his office, of all the freedmen and freedwomen who had been married while in slavery and acknowledged the relation of husband and wife towards each other; also, of the dates of their marriages and the names of their infant children; and that this acknowledgment should constitute a legal marriage and legitimate their children. No action was taken on this recommendation. To supply that want, the agent of the freedmen's bureau has caused to be made what he believes to be nearly a complete registry of all the freedmen in the state and their children, in all cases receiving the acknowledgment of both husband and wife as to their marriage. This record has cost a great deal of labor, and may hereafter be of great service. The freedmen's bureau may leave the state with these records. I am informed by the agent that he is willing to place them in the clerk's office of each county. I would advise that some act be passed requiring the clerks to receive and preserve them, and to continue the registry.

Capitol Building.

In my last annual message, I urged upon your attention the want of room in the capitol for the officers of the government and the committees and officers of the legislature, and to the insecurity of that building as a depository of the archives of the state.

I submitted to you a plan for a new building for the accommodation of the state officers and the court of appeals, and as a depository for the state archives. Room may be obtained by additions to the capitol; but owing to the combustible character of much of the materials of which the capitol is composed, I would recommend the erection of a separate building for the purposes indicated. If no appropriation for the purpose of building shall be made this year, it might be well to appoint a commission to consider and report upon the subject to the next general assembly.

Stay Law.

The law passed last winter to stay executions for debt, will expire on the first day of January, 1868. In my opinion, some action should be taken at your present session in regard to the collection of debts after the expiration of the term prescribed by the present law, in order that those interested may make arrangements accordingly. A large number of judgments have been rendered, and if executions shall be issued as soon as the law expires, great distress will be brought upon the numerous debtors in the state. If the terms of future payment shall be now prescribed, it will give those debtors time to make arrangements to discharge their debts. I have been pained to hear that many well informed men, in different parts of the state, have been discussing the subject of repudiating, in whole or in part, private debts. The discussion of this subject can be only productive of evil; it tends to weaken the sense of moral obligation, and destroy confidence between the members of the community. The charge against any man that he had refused to pay his just individual debts, whilst he retained a large amount of real and personal estate, would be offensive; yet the object seems to be to secure the passage of a general law to justify private repudiation. But this is all impossible. You cannot pass any law to impair the obligation of contracts. Devices have been resorted to in other states to shield property from sale by having valuations made, and forbidding the sale, unless the property should sell for one-half or two-thirds of the valuation. These laws have all been declared unconstitutional by the highest courts of the United States. All laws that have for their object the postponement of the collection of debts, are odious to creditors; and it is doubtful how far a law would be sustained by the courts, that exempted specified amounts of real and personal property from execution for debts contracted before the passage of the law; and there is danger in passing stay laws that look to long postponements of executions, that they may be construed by the courts to come under the constitutional prohibition against impairing the obligation of contracts. I believe the legislature has full power over the subject of priority of liens, and I think the great error in the law of last winter was, in failing to abolish the priority of judgment liens and placing all creditors upon an equal footing. The law, as it stands, has only provoked suits by the more importunate creditors. But we must now look to the future, and it strikes me that it would be wise, and perhaps the courts and creditors would concur in the measure, to direct the further stay of executions upon the payment by the debtor of the interest and twenty-five per centum of the principal within ninety days from the first day of January, 1868, and a like sum with the interest each ensuing year.

Legal Rate of Interest.

The scarcity of money in the state, makes the subject of legal interest one of paramount importance. Our usury law is almost a dead letter on the statute book. Usury, or more than six per cent. per annum, for the use of money, is charged every day in all the cities, villages and almost every neighborhood in the state. Money is worth from ten to twenty per cent., and in many instances even a higher rate of interest is exacted; but so unpopular is the plea of usury everywhere, that the business man would forfeit his credit by making it. The existence of the usury law aggravates the evil it was intended to prevent. Many good men in the state, who respect the law, will not loan money, directly or indirectly, at usurious interest, but carry their money out of the state for more profitable investment. The national banking law prohibits the banks from loaning at a greater rate of interest than that fixed by law in the state in which they are located. This prevents capital from abroad from being brought into the state for banking purposes. Thus the law tends to drive, and keep money out of the state, and the scarcity of capital forces individuals who are compelled to borrow, to obtain it from those who have no scruples about violating the law. This subject of interest is one that lies at the very foundation of our future prosperity. Manufacturers cannot get money to carry on business; farmers plough their lands, and do all the other work necessary to produce a large crop, but for want of fertilizers they receive but a scanty return for their labor. In the large grazing sections of the state the meadows are neglected, and in the pastures the grass of the field lies rotting for want of stock to eat it. It will take a long time to place the state in anything like a thrifty condition, unless the circulation of money can be stimulated by encouraging an influx of capital. It is supply and demand that regulate the price of everything. The rate of interest can only be reduced by increasing the supply of money; as long as it is worth fifteen per cent. people will pay fifteen per cent. But as soon as the supply equals the demand, or exceeds it, the rate of interest will be reduced, and then capital will seek new avenues. We are constantly

boasting of the resources of the state; but without money these resources will lie undeveloped until doomsday. Mines, manufactories
and agriculture, all languish for want of money. We must not look
for men from abroad to come and develop the resources of our state.
The people must use the means placed at their disposal to bring out
these resources, and capital must be encouraged to come in. If it
shall come in at high interest, one enterprise will start another; and
new life and energy will be infused. As soon as the farmer gets a surplus of money, he, with the merchant who has been equally successful,
will look to mining and manufacturing for investments. In a short
time that surplus will increase manufacturing establishments, and
build up cities and towns, affording diversity of employment and encouragement to everybody to work. Then the farmer will get the
highest prices for the products of his farm and pay the lowest price
for manufactured articles. Then the number of middle men will be
reduced, and as capital accumulates, the price for the use of money
will fall. The price of money is always cheapest where all the necessaries of life, and of manufacture and agriculture are in the greatest
proximity. It is believed that ten or twelve per cent. would be a sufficient rate of interest to retain the capital already in the state, and
encourage capitalists abroad to send it in for investment. I would recommend that where no contract is made, six per cent. should be the
legal interest, but that a higher rate be allowed by contract in writing.

County Roads and County Levies.

Our road law, and the laws regulating levies for county expenses,
need revision. By law all the county levy may be raised by what is
termed a " poll tax," and in many instances is thus raised. All male
persons over sixteen years of age, without reference to color, are subject to the county levy and poor tax. This tax is particularly oppressive and unjust to the laboring classes. I have heard complaints
from counties this year, where the county and poor tax amounted in
some instances to five, in others to six dollars for each poll. The
taxing of minors between the ages of 16 and 21 years, is a violation
of every principle of law. By law the minor is not the disposer of
his own time, nor has he the legal power to make contracts or dispose of his property. The same class of persons upon whom the
county and poor levies are assessed, except such as are over sixty

years of age, are required to make and keep in repair the county roads, and may be ordered out for that purpose ten or twenty days of the year. I have seen instances, under this law, where a man owning no real estate, and dependent upon his daily labor, with three or four sons and apprentices between the ages of 16 and 21 years, has been required to work on the public highways from five to fifteen days of the year, besides paying a county levy on himself, apprentices and children. In the same neighborhood, men owning ten and twenty thousand dollars worth of real estate, whose teams were constantly using these roads, but who were over 60 years of age, were exempted by law from work on the highways, their lands and other property not assessed for the county levy, and themselves only paying. for county objects a single poll tax. These instances are common all over the state. It is to be said, however, to the credit of some counties, that they have raised a portion of their levy from a tax on property subject to state taxation. A law that is so often and so flagrantly abused as this is, ought to be repealed at once. I would recommend that all laws pertaining to this subject be repealed, and an act passed to place the burden of the county and poor levies on property made liable to taxation by the state, and further providing that all male persons over the age of 21 years shall pay a poll tax for county objects not exceeding the tax assessed upon two or three hundred dollars worth of property, and that the roads be worked under the superintendence of a commissioner. Thus the laboring classes will have the opportunity of paying their county and poor levy by labor on the roads. The county and poor levy system, as it now stands, has driven many a laboring man, who would have been a valuable citizen, from the state. As labor is the foundation of all wealth and progress, every one that can be induced to come into the state to labor, is a valuable addition to her resources, whilst every one of such persons who leaves, is a serious loss. It is not wise to continue upon your statute book laws which oppress that class. The agents of the freedmen's bureau have called my attention to this subject of county and poll levies, alleging its injustice as constituting a reason for their interposition to prevent the collection of these taxes from the freedmen. Although they regard the tax as unjust, yet they have advised the colored people in all cases to pay the tax, hoping that the legislature will alter the law.

Schools and Colleges.

It is deeply to be regretted that the state, on account of its financial condition, cannot contribute to the general education of her children. The common school is the nursery in which the young mind is trained for energetic action and for future usefulness. The state that neglects the common school, sanctions ignorance and indolence, which, sooner or later, bring paralysis on her energies. This neglect on the part of our state has been one of the causes why so many of her able-bodied men have left Virginia and gone to other states, where their children have greater advantages. Our colleges and university are reported to be in a flourishing condition. The Military institute and the University of Virginia, from their origin, have been the recipients of munificent annual donations from the treasury of the state. Other colleges are holders of a considerable amount of state bonds. If the education of the poor children of the state is left unprovided for, what justice is there in taxing the laboring class, together with the wealthy, for the benefit only of the classes whose sons are sent to the colleges and the University? The state should be just before it is generous. Widows and the guardians of orphans are holders of state bonds on which depend their hopes for bread, yet they are not paid one cent; but the bonds they hold are taxed to support the higher institutions of learning. Many of them are forced to sell a portion of their bonds for forty cents in the dollar, to buy the necessaries of life. It is true that strong arguments are urged in favor of contributions on behalf of the state to the university, the institute and the colleges; but these appeals are not nearly so strong as the appeal of the poor man's child and the destitute orphan, who have no school provided for them! But they have no eloquent and influential advocates as the son of the rich man has, in the persons of professors of colleges, to press their claims before the general assembly. It is very doubtful whether the power should be exercised by the legislature to tax the masses to support a college or university; there is no general compensation derived by the state from such appropriations, in theory or in practice. The student who enters the college, goes there for his own benefit—to prepare himself for some one of the professions, or to acquire a classical education, with its accomplishments, that he may better enjoy his fortune. The argument that a public compensation is derived from the arrangement that some of these students are to be gratuitously educated as teachers, is founded more in idea than in fact. I suppose some of these persons do teach for short periods; but few, if any of them, ever become teachers of the poor. I have lived in this, my native state, nearly all my life, and I have never yet seen a graduate of the University or of the Military institute teaching a common school. There are, I doubt not, a few honorable exceptions, in which these professed charities are bestowed upon meritorious young men who could not otherwise attend the seats of learning; but it will be found that in most instances the sons of influential men, who are not in needy circumstances, obtain these places. The honors, rewards and comforts attendant upon the successful practice of the learned professions have always held out sufficient incentives to young men of every grade to enter and fill their ranks to repletion. Men skilled in the mechanic arts, and in agricultural, mining and manufacturing pursuits, are greatly needed in the state; but no premium is offered to assist the apprentice to learn his trade, or the farmer's, mechanic's or laborer's son to become a proficient in those pursuits which conduce so much to the greatness of a people. This whole idea of taxing the poorer and middle classes to support colleges and universities, whilst the education of these classes is unprovided for by the state, is founded on a false dogma. It is like commencing to build a church at the steeple instead of the foundation. It will be found that in this country, in all the states where common schools have been provided for all the children and the colleges left to private enterprise, both colleges and schools have attained the greatest efficiency. It is urged that by giving state aid to our higher institutions of learning, we encourage the education of our young men in the state, and thereby retain the money which would otherwise go abroad. This is true; but we have always sent more money out of the state to purchase hay and butter alone, which could have been produced by our own farmers, than would support all our colleges. Why not, then, offer a premium on the production of butter and hay; and so with various other articles we ought to produce, but which are brought from abroad?

In my last annual message I made a statement of the condition of the Literary fund, showing that, for any practical purposes, we have no longer a Literary fund. That statement was controverted

before the general assembly last winter, by an attempt to show that
we had one million, six hundred and eighteen thousand, fifty-seven
dollars and five cents, invested in the same securities in which it was
invested in 1860. This is true; but of what does this investment
consist? It is in old James river stock, old military six per cents,
bank loan of 1814, loan to the commonwealth, and internal improvement loan. The only show of value that can be attached to these
securities is to be found in the fact that they exist on the statute
book, and not one cent can possibly be realized from any of them,
except by direct tax on the people. Up to 1861 between two and
three hundred thousand dollars of this fund were invested in bank
stocks, which yielded a dividend; the whole of the balance had been
so managed that it was lost, as far as permanent securities were concerned; but its payment was endorsed by the state, and the people
were taxed, annually, for every cent expended for literary purposes,
except the dividends derived from the banks. And yet, the idea was
held out to the people, from year to year, that we had a "Literary
fund" of over two millions of dollars, from which dividends were
derived; and an annual payment was made to schools and colleges
out of these pretended dividends, which, as I have shown, came directly from the pockets of the people. The "Literary fund" is a
myth. It once existed, but it is squandered, and can no more be
reckoned among the assets of the state than can a fortune spent be
left as a legacy to the children of its former owner. It is useless to
attempt to legislate about a thing that has no existence. In this case
it must be set down to the account of "profit and loss." It was not
lost by the war—except the small amount of bank stock—it was gone
before. When, therefore, you expend money for literary purposes,
you should not order the payment to be made out of the "Literary
fund," but you should simply and truthfully direct it to be paid out
of "any moneys in the public treasury not otherwise appropriated,"
and for which a tax must be levied.

The subject of the education of the freedmen is attracting great
and deserved attention all over the country. It is admitted on all
hands, that if the freedman shall be made a valuable member of the
community, it must be done by affording him the means of intellectual culture. I am gratified to be able to state that considerable
sums of money have been raised by benevolent societies of the North
for this purpose, and that a number of schools for the education of

freedmen are in successful operation in this city and elsewhere in the state. It is proper and just to these benevolent associations to add, that in addition to the freedmen's schools provided by them, the soldier's aid society of the North have established in this city schools for white children, provided with competent teachers, which are now prospering, and where upwards of three hundred children are gratuitously taught.

Agricultural Land Scrip.

In compliance with the act of the general assembly at your last session, directing an agent to be appointed to receive the land scrip donated by congress for the erection of an agricultural college, I appointed W. B. Isaacs, Esq., of Richmond city, the agent to receive and sell this scrip. He has given the matter the requisite attention; but owing to the press of business in the Department of the Interior at Washington, the commissioner has been, as yet, unable to deliver the scrip, though I believe it is now nearly ready for delivery.

It may become your duty at the present session, to designate the location of the institution which shall receive the benefit of this donation. William & Mary college is now without proper buildings to carry on successfully its operations. I am in great hopes that you will make it the interest of that institution to change its location to this city, by adding to its present endowment the proceeds of the sale of the lands donated by congress. I think it would be grateful to the feelings of the friends and alumni of that ancient seat of learning to see it transferred to the metropolis of the state. With this rich endowment, it would be placed in a condition to resume its former high place among the literary institutions of the country, and perhaps to equal its former renown. It would be necessary, of course, to change to some extent the course of instruction, in order to make it the great polytechnic school contemplated by the munificence of congress, and so much needed by the state. I have seen no reason to change the views in regard to this subject, presented in my last annual message, which I again submit for your consideration. "In my opinion the college to which this donation should be applied, should be located in the city of Richmond, which is central and easily accessible from all parts of the state. It should be a polytechnic school, teaching modern languages, mathematics, natural philosophy, mechanics, engineering, mineralogy, geology, vegetable and mineral chemistry; and chairs of design, botany and agriculture, with military tactics to complete the list. The farm should embrace about 300 acres, which would afford ample room for the culture of the vine, and the ascertainment of all its choice varieties adapted to our climate. Fruits should be cultivated with the arts of grafting and dwarfing. The cereals and root crops should have their place, and opportunity afforded for the application of all the fertilizers. All the berries should receive their full share of attention. The school should have no vacation, and if possible, the course of instruction should extend to five scholastic years. Three months, from July to October, should be spent in the field with their tents and the full corps of professors. This would afford ample opportunity for the practical application of all their studies. The state, with its agriculture, botany, mineralogy, geology and geography, would afford an ample field for investigation to the corps of teachers and pupils. This is what our state eminently needs at this time. The young men of Virginia are equal in intellect to those of any state or nation. Their education heretofore, has consisted in the routine of the old collegiate course, fitting them for stump speaking, politics, law and medicine—all well enough in their places—but it has not qualified them for developing the true wealth of our great commonwealth, blessed as she is in a more productive soil, and abounding with a greater variety of mineral ores than any other state in the Union. This school should be metropolitan in its location. The people come from all parts of the state to her metropolis; the great state school should be there. Its development and perfections, in all things taught there, should be where the people could see them. There would then be encouragement for emulation and progress. It would be the great light of the state in all that would be taught there."

The Lunatic and Deaf and Dumb Asylums.

These benevolent institutions, dispensing their blessings to the hundreds who are recipients of their ministrations; are well known to you. They are the asylums of the unfortunate and afflicted, and the good they are constantly dispensing, recommend their liberal encouragement to your favorable consideration. The reports of the officers of these institutions are herewith transmitted.

Emigration.

The subject of labor is attracting great attention in the state. We must first depend upon the native labor now in the state, white and colored. This is to be encouraged by the repeal of oppressive laws, by the encouragement of common schools, and by fair wages and kind treatment. The colored man has great odds against him. In many instances he is paid less wages than the white man, in the same field, and required to do the same amount of work. If he does not, he is denounced as worthless : he has the theories of politicians and the dogmas of divines against him; the one class maintaining that the true theory of the organization of society is, that capital should own labor; and the other, proving to their own satisfaction, from the sacred record, that God in his wisdom made the negro for a slave—that he is the laborer to be owned and worked for his own amelioration and advancement, and the general good of the few who should own slaves. Men are attached to their theories—by these kings rule by Divine right. The negro has to progress, if progress he shall, against theories. In some sections of the state he has done well this year. He ought to have a fair chance; and it may be, when he shall have as many inducements to work as the white man, he will work. There are few who toil all day but cast a wistful eye at the setting sun. The negro should be tried hopefully; and I am pleased to find that a large number of the best men of the state are willing to encourage the freedman to work, and give him a fair chance, as regards wages and education.

The next hope for labor is from foreign emigration. I have given much thought to this subject, in connection with the various schemes set on foot or projected for its encouragement. There are three classes of emigrants now seeking the United States from Europe. The first are those who have heard of our cheap and productive lands, who are tenants or owners of small farms in their own country. These people, inspired by a natural desire to own homes, are fleeing from a system of tenantry to a better country, with small means to bear expenses and purchase homesteads. The second class is composed of a good class of young men, inured to labor, who come to procure work and to better their condition. They will accompany the first class and be apt to adopt the same section if they can get employment. The third class is composed of the inmates of work-houses, alms-houses, prisons and the purlieus of the cities, who have earned a precarious livelihood by their wits and vices.

To attract the first and second classes to our state, we will have to present the inducement they desire—homes and employment. To attract the third, by paying large sums of money to the emigrant agents, as a reward upon each head brought here, so that the amount of money they get depends upon the number they bring, will drain the influx from the almshouses, workhouses, prisons and gutters of Europe, into the state, each individual to become, in time, a pauper or convict here. Great efforts are being made to induce the legislature to appropriate money to emigration societies. I do not think that it would be good policy to make these appropriations, nor would I favor any organization to which the state shall be a party, where money is to be paid out of the public treasury in proportion to the number of emigrants imported. It will certainly lead to filling the state with a pauper population. The inducement for the better class of emigration must be left, to a great extent, to individual enterprise. Last winter the legislature authorized the appointment of three commissioners of emigration. They have been appointed, and the board is organized. It is believed that this board may be made the channel through which individuals may procure tenants, laborers and purchasers for their lands. But it will require active co-operation on the part of individuals to effect this object. In the office of the board will be kept a faithful registry of all the lands in the state offered for sale, on the prescribed conditions. Parties in the state, desiring purchasers through this channel, should have their lands carefully laid off with plats, showing the amount of land in each lot proposed to be sold, designating the county in which it is located, its distance from the county seat, proximity to railroads or navigable water courses, and the distance from the nearest general market; the amount and quality of timber, the amount of cleared land, the character and productiveness of the soil, and whether best fitted for agriculture, horticulture or grazing; and the price per acre at which it is offered. In all cases the title should be unencumbered, and a certificate of the clerk of the county court to that effect should be produced, with a certificate of the county surveyor, as to the reasonableness of the price compared with other lands in the same section, and the truthfulness of the description. These descriptions should be recorded in the books kept by the commissioners, and printed from time to time in the languages of the countries in which they are designed to be used. In the Tidewater districts, where the lands are adapted to horticulture, and can be laid off into small tracts, particular care should be taken to leave roads and outlets. I think the legislature ought to make an appropriation to defray the expenses of printing, and of a clerk to the commissioners to perform the labor required in their office. The publication of these advertisements of lands might be made quarterly; and when any land is so offered, the price should not be changed before the next publication, and then, at the instance of the owner, it might be reduced or enhanced. The executive, then, could append his certificate as to the truthfulness of the descriptions, values and titles. These descriptions could be freely circulated, and would receive credit abroad. The owners of the lands in particular sections could place these publications in the hands of emigrant associations, and make such terms in regard to their sales as might be agreed on. This board should also receive and record in like manner, propositions from persons who desire to lease lands. This would bring the lands of the state practically to the attention of emigrants from all parts of the world, and would offer homes to those who wish either to buy or rent. These persons would naturally be accompanied by a fair proportion of common laborers. The advantages of this plan must be evident to every owner of real estate who has more land than he can work.

Geological Survey.

It is of the greatest importance that we shall have a geological survey of the state, which should include a full description of its mineral and botanical productions. The want of such a survey is greatly felt. I have had frequent applications for such a work for distribution in this country and in Europe. It would not be expensive, and it is only in this way that our valuable mineral deposits and varied vegetable productions can be brought fully to public attention. There is not a county in the state, from the seaboard to our western border, but would be greatly compensated for the outlay required for such a work. It is believed that eight or ten thousand dollars annually would be sufficient to procure competent men to complete the survey in two, or, at most, three years.

Artificial Limbs.

The close of the rebellion found a large number of persons who had lost one or more of their limbs on the field of battle. Many of these persons are poor, and were, before the war, dependent upon their daily labor for the support of themselves and their families. They are now unable to work and have no means of supplying themselves with artificial limbs, which would, in very many instances, enable them to work for a livelihood. The medical association of this city has taken a lively and most commendable interest in this subject, collecting information as to the number and circumstances of this unfortunate class of men, and of the best and most economical mode of supplying artificial limbs. The association has prepared a memorial on this subject, to be presented to your body, for which I ask your serious and favorable consideration. As a matter of economy, I am satisfied that an appropriation in aid of the object would be wise, as there are many of these men dependent on the community for the support of themselves and families, who, if supplied with artificial limbs, would be enabled to labor for themselves, and thus rid the counties and corporations of the burden of their support. As a plan of beneficence, it commends itself to every generous heart.

Fence Law.

I think the law passed last winter on the subject of enclosures, has not given general satisfaction. I am satisfied that the true interests of the state require that all "fence laws" should be repealed, and the subject left to the provisions of the common law. I believe the people in the Tide-water and Piedmont sections of the state are ready for such a change. I doubt whether the people of the Valley and West are prepared for it. Having always been accustomed to fences, our people have not fully estimated the vast expense of keeping them up, and the advantages to be derived from the employment of herdsmen. I see no objection to the repeal of the law so far as it applies to the Tide-water and Piedmont sections, and leaving the subject, as at present, to the discretion of the courts in the Valley and western counties. I commend the subject to your attention.

James River Canal.

At the last meeting of the stockholders of this company, it was resolved to reduce the tolls on minerals, timber and hay. This, at last, is a step in the right direction. The tolls heretofore have been so high, that the trade in those leading articles has received no encouragement. The canal leads into a region in which there are some of the most valuable iron deposits in the world : encouraged by low tolls, I have no doubt that iron manufacturers will find it to their interest to erect their furnaces in the great coal fields on the line of the canal, near Richmond, and bring their ore from the deposits above: this will stimulate that great branch of industry. Large beds of kaoline lie near the canal, which will doubtless contribute their share to its commerce. Active steps are being taken to enlarge the manufacture of hydraulic lime on the line of the canal: it is believed that 160,000 barrels will be produced annually. Competent engineers have pronounced the hydraulic lime manufactured on James river, unequalled by any produced elsewhere in the United States. The transportation of common lime will also contribute largely to the business of this canal. It is hoped that the stimulus thus given to other business, by the development of the production and manufacture of these leading articles, will amply compensate for the reduction fixed upon.

Railroads.

One of the great objects of our railroad system was to develop the material interests of the commonwealth, by facilitating and cheapening travel and the transportation of our products from distant points to market ; also, to afford lines for the transportation of passengers and freight in connection with other lines without the state. To make these improvements, about twenty millions of our public debt was incurred. In nearly all these roads the state owns three-fifths of the stock, in addition to bonds for money loaned for their construction and equipment. It is one of the highest duties of the representatives of the people to see that the vast power created by the public money is not used to the public detriment, but that the greatest benefit to the state shall be derived therefrom.

From the construction of a railroad in any particular locality, it is impossible that the people in parts of the country remote from its line

can derive any direct benefit. The justice of the claim for a general
contribution, by all the tax payers, to construct these improvements
is based on the idea that they will enhance the value of real estate,
and create additional personal property, thereby increasing the subjects of taxation and the value of taxable property in their neighborhood, and thus reduce the amount of taxes to be paid by the residents
in more remote localities. They should be the great arteries of the
commerce of the state to supply and build up her cities, which are
the depositories of that wealth, which is a fruitful source of taxation.
Our cities pay a very large proportion of our taxes. Yet, strange as
it may appear, freight and passengers have been carried from beyond
the limits of the state, through its entire territory, to distant points,
paying in some instances little over half the rates charged from our
cities to the same points. In some instances our manufacturers have
had to ship their goods out of the state, and then have them re-
shipped to pass over our own roads to their original destination, in
order to place them on an equality as to charges for transportation,
with articles going from other states. It is easy to be seen that
by this system, our most enterprising manufacturers and wholesale
merchants will be forced to leave the state and go to other cities where
they can carry on business under better auspices, and thus the management of our railroads will defeat the very object of their construction. Each of these companies is an independent corporation, with
certain vested rights; each claims supremacy in its sphere, affecting an
inclination to do as it pleases in regard to its connections and through
and local tolls. Hence we hear frequent complaints that one company
throws obstructions in the way of another in regard to connections,
rates of tolls, fares, transhipments, exchange of cars, &c. It is charged
that the excuse for these high local rates, is that the goods have to be
carried; that the roads are in a necessitous condition, and must make
all they can out of the necessities of those who are compelled to use
them. It is in the power of the general assembly to correct these
irregularities, if not abuses. It is not competent for the legislature
to pass an act declaring that any particular road shall charge a specific
rate of tolls on freight or passengers. But this object can be attained
by general legislation. The law now prescribes a maximum rate. It
is right, as a general rule, that a higher rate should be paid on short
than on long distances. The leading lines through the state, carrying
passengers and freight to and from distant points outside of her limits,

come into competition with other leading lines, passing through other states to and from the same points. By these lines competition is produced and tolls are reduced to their lowest remunerative rates. Through tolls, established in connection with other companies, should constitute the basis for the charge for what are called "local tolls," or tolls from one point to another on the same road. As most of these roads form continuous lines through the state, their tariffs of tolls for passengers and freight should be uniform; so that passengers and freight, from one line to another, should not be subject at points of intersection to new conditions and new charges for handling freight. For the purpose of carrying out this idea, I propose that the Norfolk and Petersburg, Southside, Danville, and Virginia and Tennessee roads should constitute one road; the Virginia and Tennessee, Orange and Alexandria, and Virginia Central should constitute one road; the Petersburg and Weldon, Richmond and Petersburg, Richmond connection, and Richmond, Fredericksburg and Potomac roads should constitute one road. When transportation is required at any depot on any of these roads, it should be received and transported to any depot on any other road connecting therewith, that may be desired, at a uniform rate of charges, on the basis above stated, and tickets, checks and bills of lading given accordingly; and for any loss or damage sustained in transportation, the party injured should have his right of action against any company over whose road the passage was so contracted for. It is believed that one cent per ton per mile for freight, and one cent per mile for each passenger, for short distances, over the rates charged on through rates, would be adequate compensation where freight or passengers pass over the entire length of the road, or merchandize or manufactures from any of the principal cities are transported, they should be placed on an equal footing with through freight and passengers.

For illustration: I have proposed that the Norfolk and Petersburg, Southside, Danville and Virginia and Tennessee roads, for the purposes of the proposed act, shall be considered one road. Then consider the line from Norfolk to Bristol the whole length of one road. From Bristol to Alexandria will be considered the length of another road. For the purposes of graduation, each should be laid off into ten sections; then, freight starting at Norfolk and transported one-tenth of the distance, would be charged one cent per mile over through freight. If it should pass over two sections, two mills should be dropped from the additional charge, and so on; dropping a mill for each section to the end of the line. Where goods are hauled by the car-load, for short distances, should this rate bring the charge for transportation, below eight dollars per car-load of eight tons, the company should be allowed to charge such reasonable sum as may be agreed on. Of course all articles in packages of less than a ton's weight, should be charged on the same basis with like articles carried through. The act should further provide that the tariff of rates, on all these railroads, should be made out and signed by the president and superintendent of each road; a copy furnished to the Board of public works, and placed at each depot in some conspicuous place, where it may be seen by every person desiring to use the road as is now required by law. There are articles, such as minerals, lumber, stock, hay, &c., that these companies may be able to carry at less than schedule rates, the reduction depending upon the amount to be transported, and the dispatch with which the cars are loaded and unloaded. Privilege should be given to transport these, by contract, at less than tariff rates; but these special contracts should be uniform, and in no instance should a greater charge per ton per mile be allowed on long distances than short ones.

. I am aware that some of our railroad companies claim that, under their chartered rights, the legislature cannot legally reduce their tolls until they shall have declared a certain dividend on their stock. This is true; but it is also true, that both by law and by custom, they are common carriers; and as such, they are subject to legislative action. I do not propose that you shall fix the rates of their tariffs; I propose that they shall fix them on the through freights, which shall be the basis for the charges on home freights. There can be no question as to the power of the legislature to enforce this condition. This appears to me the best arrangement that can be made by law for the present.

Last winter, the working of the Norfolk and Petersburg and Southside roads was placed under the same management. The number of employees was at once reduced; the rolling stock of both roads was made more efficient; and the working expenses of the Southside road were reduced fifty per cent. I was in great hopes that we would be able to consolidate the working of the Virginia and Tennessee road with the two last named roads, thereby making one great connecting line from Norfolk to Bristol—a distance of over four hundred miles

If this had been done, there can be no doubt that in the course of two or three years, the income of these roads would have been not less than four millions of dollars. Short lines of railroad can never be made profitable, except under most favorable circumstances. Situated as ours are, the working, to be remunerative, must be consolidated. The most casual observer can comprehend, that working these roads under one general supervision, will be productive of economy in every way. The amount of rolling stock, number of employees, shop expenses, &c., will all be greatly diminished, thereby increasing the net earnings of the roads. This would enable the roads to lower the rate of tolls, thus stimulating industry by encouraging the production of additional articles for transportation. This subject is thoroughly understood by railroad men everywhere. In states where railroads have not received state aid, but have been left to private enterprise, these short roads, worked independently, have failed, and gone under the auctioneer's hammer, passing into the hands of companies who have consolidated their working with continuous lines of other roads, when they became profitable. Had not our roads been backed by the great power of the state, they would have been exposed to sale before their completion. Now, that the state is unable to render them further aid, in consequence of the heavy debt already incurred, they are borrowing money at ruinous rates of interest, each one going into the market upon its own responsibility. Capitalists well understand that short lines of road, worked independently, cannot be made profitable: hence we see what we deem good bonds, bearing eight per cent. interest, netting to the companies where a loan can be effected, little over eighty cents in the dollar. If all our roads were consolidated and put under the management of one or two intelligent heads, there is no reason why their bonds should not become as good as seven-thirty bonds of the United States in any market. But to defeat this object, leading men from different parts of the state were brought to the capital, and retained to attend the meeting of the stockholders of the Virginia and Tennessee road, where the whole scheme was denounced as an infringement of the franchises of the company, and as an innovation upon the customs of Virginia, and other arguments about as reasonable, urged upon the private stockholders. Thus the scheme was defeated. It was gravely contended that this subject ought to be submitted to the legislature, and that you should take action before the companies should act. I confess that I see only one way by which the legislature can accomplish the purpose: that is, to repeal the law which scales the vote of the state, and instruct her proxies to vote for consolidating the management of the roads.

The York river road, which was totally destroyed, is in process of reconstruction, and will soon be in working condition.

I regret that I cannot give so flattering a report of the condition of the Manassas Gap road. My opinion is, that it should be transferred on some conditions, to the Orange and Alexandria company, which it is hoped, will in a short time be in a condition to enable them to complete it, and work it in connection with their road. The city of Alexandria has a large interest in this work.

The Virginia and Kentucky railroad company has been re-organized, with R. W. Hughes, Esq., as its president. It is to be hoped that by his energy and intelligent management this important road will be completed. This road will form a connecting link between the Virginia and Tennessee and two important roads through Kentucky to Cumberland Gap—the one from Cincinnati, and the other from Louisville, both in progress of construction, which will give continuous communication between that fertile region of country and the Atlantic seaboard in Virginia.

The commissioners appointed at your last session to procure a company to construct the Covington and Ohio road, will, I suppose, report their action directly to the legislature. This road, in my opinion, offers the greatest inducement for the investment of capital, of any railroad project in the country. It is attracting the attention of a number of capitalists in the northwest, and the east, and I am confident that its construction will soon be undertaken.

I indulge the hope that the Danville railroad company will consider it to be their interest to complete the Roanoke Valley road, which will form a very important feeder to their valuable improvement, and secure the trade of the rich Roanoke Valley to Richmond.

The Newport's News road has been commenced, with a flattering prospect of speedy completion.

I do not know what legislation may be needed in regard to these roads, to better their condition; but I have no doubt the subject will receive due consideration at your hands.

Berkeley and Jefferson.

I herewith transmit the report of the attorney general, to which I respectfully refer you, for information as to the action taken in regard to the status of Berkeley and Jefferson. There are also some important facts stated in regard to the oyster law, and other subjects, to which you are respectfully referred.

Political.

On the 16th of June last, the Secretary of State of the United States forwarded to me an official copy of a joint resolution of congress, proposing an amendment to the constitution of the United States, which it is my duty to submit to the general assembly. It is in the following words, viz:

Be it resolved by the senate and house of representatives of the United States of America in congress assembled, (two-thirds of both houses concurring,) That the following article be proposed to the legislatures of the several states as an amendment to the constitution of the United States, which, when ratified by three-fourths of said legislatures, shall be valid as part of the constitution, namely :

ARTICLE XIV.

SECTION 1. All persons born or naturalized in the United States and subject to the jurisdiction thereof, are citizens of the United States and of the state wherein they reside. No state shall make or enforce any law which shall abridge the privileges or immunities of citizens of the United States ; nor shall any state deprive any person of life, liberty or property, without due process of law, nor deny to any person within its jurisdiction the equal protection of the laws.

SECTION 2. Representatives shall be apportioned among the several states according to their respective numbers, counting the whole number of persons in each state, excluding Indians not taxed. But when the right to vote at any election for the choice of electors for President and Vice President of the United States, representatives in congress, the executive and judicial officers of a state, or the members of the legislature thereof, is denied to any of the male inhabitants of such state, being twenty-one years of age and citizens of the United States, or in any way abridged, except for participation in rebellion or other crime, the basis of representation therein shall be reduced in the proportion which the number of such male citizens shall bear to the whole number of male citizens twenty-one years of age in such state.

SECTION 3. No person shall be a senator or representative in congress, or elector of president and vice president, or hold any office, civil or military, under the United States, or under any state, who, having previously taken an oath as a member of congress, or as an officer of the United States, or as a member of any state legislature, or as an executive or judicial officer of any state, to support the constitution of the United States, shall have engaged in insurrection or rebellion against the same, or given aid and comfort to the enemies thereof; but congress may, by a vote of two-thirds of each house, remove such disability.

SECTION 4. The validity of the public debt of the United States, authorized by law, including debts incurred for payment of pensions and bounties for services in suppressing insurrection and rebellion, shall not be questioned; but neither the United States nor any state shall assume or pay any debt or obligation incurred in aid of insurrection or rebellion against the United States, or any claim for the loss or emancipation of any slave; but all such debts, obligations or claims, shall be held illegal and void.

SECTION 5. The congress shall have power to enforce, by appropriate legislation, the provisions of this article.

> SCHUYLER COLFAX, Speaker House of Rep.
> LAFÁYETTE S. FOSTER, President Senate, *pro tem.*

Attest:

> EDWARD MCPHERSON, Clerk House of Rep.
> J. W. FORNEY, Secretary of Senate.

There is no ambiguity in the language of the proposed amendment: it is before you for your mature consideration—for adoption or rejection: you are fully acquainted with all the circumstances which led to its proposal. The congress of the United States has made its acceptance a condition precedent to the admission of representatives, in the councils of the nation, from states now unrepresented.

The President of the United States disapproved of this amendment, and insisted on the immediate admission into congress, from all the unrepresented states, of such representatives as were "*loyal,*" who had been elected according to the forms of law. What he means by the term "*loyal,*" is a subject of controversy. A number of his friends have explicitly affirmed, that he meant only such as could truthfully take the oath prescribed by congress, to be taken by all persons before entering upon the duties of any office under the government of the United States. It is claimed by a majority of congress and those who support them, that the people of the states now unrepresented, voluntarily withdrew their representatives from the councils of the nation, and attempted to set up an independent government or confederation, and thereby inaugurated a great civil war; that the people in those states have committed a grave offence, and as security for the future, the congress of the United States has authority to prescribe the terms on which they shall be readmitted to representation, and to determine by constitutional provisions, that certain persons shall be disqualified from holding federal or state offices, as a punishment for having participated in the rebellion.

On this great question, of such vast interest to the people of ten states, a clearly defined separation took place between the President and the congress of the United States. Each appealed to the people of the twenty-six states now represented, to decide the controversy at the late elections. The elections are over, and a very decisive majority has been rendered in favor of the congressional view of the subject.

Three points—as the controversy is susceptible of analysis, as I understand it—were distinctly submitted and decided at these elections, viz:

First: That the unrepresented states shall not gain additional political power in the congress of the United States by reason of the manumission of the slaves, where the right of suffrage in those states is withheld from the negro population.

Second: That persons who have heretofore held executive, legislative or judicial offices under the government of the United States, or of any state, and have engaged in the late civil war against the United States, shall not be eligible to like places without the consent of two-thirds of congress.

Third: That the terms upon which representatives shall be readmitted to congress from the states lately in rebellion, and disabilities imposed on or removed from those who participated in that rebellion, shall be prescribed by congress and not by the President.

There is an effort being made at the North and in the South, by politicians who support the President's policy, to induce the legislatures of the non-represented states to reject the constitutional amendment, in the hope that in another contest before the people, they may be more successful; and they predict a violent conflict between the executive and legislative branches of the general government, by means of which he may obtain the majority in congress. But when we consider the favorable auspices for the President's policy under which the late political contest was inaugurated—he having been elected by the party which now opposes him, supported by able cabinet officers, and some of the shrewdest politicians of the country of the same party, in the hope of dividing that party by means of the power and patronage of the federal government, in some instances bestowing that patronage on former political friends, in others, persuasively holding out the emoluments of office to be conferred after the election—and that in opposition to all this the President has been defeated, it is not likely that another campaign can be so favorably inaugurated for the supposed interests of the southern states as the one just closed.

The people of the South ought not again to be beguiled by the promises of these professed allies and friends at the North. The same promises were made in 1860 and 1861; I need not remind you how they were fulfilled. It is wise to look at the material, as well as numbers of which a party is composed, from which aid or support is expected. That party which supports the President at the North, numbers in its ranks many wealthy and intelligent men; it has also a small portion of what may be termed the middle class—substantial people. But its great numerical strength lies amongst the most ignorant classes, and those representing the least property. You have in this party, then, those who aspire to be the aristocracy of wealth and refinement, supported, for the most part, in the large cities, by the poorest class. A party composed as this is, cannot be relied upon in case of a physical contest. The wealthy are timid, and cling to their capital; the greater portion of the residue of the party being poor and ignorant, shrink from the contest for want of interest, looking at little beyond their physical security.

The congressional party is composed of a large class, the equals in wealth and intelligence of the leaders of the party of the President; by the middle classes, amongst whom are distributed by far the greater portion of the property and intelligence of the country, and by the independent laboring classes of the manufacturing and agricultural districts. It now embraces the flower and strength of both the old political parties in the northern states, brought together by the late war, and now held together by a common sentiment and sympathy. Young men arriving at the age of manhood, naturally fall into, and thus swell its ranks. It will become stronger for many years to come. This may be termed the *dominant* party, led by the ardent and cultivated intellects now representing it in congress. A glance

at the details of the late elections will convince the most sceptical of
the correctness of the views as to the composition of the two parties
above taken.

The great Atlantic cities are old, and have been aptly termed the
great ulcers of the body politic.   The lower classes there live on excitement, and are mostly controlled by their passions and prejudices,
(except where they are intelligently employed in healthy manufacturing establishments) ; there government patronage is lavishly dis-
pensed, and there the President finds his greatest strength.   As you
approach the great agricultural and manufacturing districts, where
education is as common as children—where the people read and
think—you find the great strength of the congressional party.

The practical question for your consideration now is, whether, by
the rejection of the proposed constitutional amendment, you are likely
to place *the people* of our state in a better condition.   If the views I
have presented be correct, there is no hope of better terms.   It is
urged that it would be dishonorable to accept the terms offered in the
amendment.   I think this objection is not substantial.   There was
no political power acquired by the surrender of the confederate armies.   The terms were, as to the soldier, the surrender of his arms,
giving his parol that he would go to his home and remain there peaceably until exchanged as a prisoner of war, or released from his parol;
the officer had more liberal terms granted him, but these terms were
only such as applied to a prisoner of war, in a military point of
view.   This position is fully confirmed by the fact, that after one of
the federal commanders had attempted to give a political status to
a large division of the insurgent army, the political feature of the
treaty was ordered to be stricken out by the government at Washington.

Up to this point, no political status had been given to those who
had been engaged in levying war against the government.   It is not
material to the argument whether the unrepresented states are to be
regarded as members of a de facto government, which had been over-
thrown by the arms of the United States, or as an aggregate of individuals who had been engaged in rebellion against the government,
which had been suppressed.   If these Confederate States are regarded
as a de facto *government*, they had surrendered and were at the discretion of the conqueror.   If we regard the inhabitants as persons
who were engaged in domestic violence and waging war against the

United States, they were subdued and were amenable to the laws.
The President of the United States regarded them in the latter capacity, and decided that all the state governments in the unrepresented
states (except Virginia, Tennessee, Louisiana and Arkansas, where
governments had been re-established by the loyal people,) had been
abolished by this "domestic violence." He ordered conventions to
be called to make new organic laws or constitutions for those states,
prescribing who should and who should not vote for delegates to these
conventions. He issued a proclamation, enumerating some thirteen
or fourteen classes of persons liable to the penal laws of the United
States unless they should obtain his special pardon. Thus he attempted to fix the political status of these states.

The term of the thirty-eighth congress expired on the 3d of March,
1865; the surrender of the confederate armies took place in the
months of April and May following, and the action of the President
to which I have just referred was had before the assembling of the
present congress in December of the same year. When congress assembled, it in effect denied the validity of the action of the President
in attempting to define the political status of the people of the unrepresented states, who had been engaged in levying war against the
government, and denied admission to representatives from those states
unless they should adopt the proposed amendment. Nor has congress sanctioned the validity of the President's action so far, except
by acquiescence, and on condition that this constitutional amendment shall be adopted by the legislature of each state. It is claimed
by congress, that being the law-making branch of the government, it
belongs to that body to determine the political status of the people of
those states. Therefore, as yet, the political status of the people in
those states is precisely in the same condition that it was on the day
the confederate armies were surrendered. There has been nothing
done by the law-making power of the government of the United
States to settle that question, except the submission of this proposition to amend the constitution.

The people of those states, as a conquered nation, or as individuals
who have forfeited their political rights by rebellion, are still under
the ban of the government, or in the power of the conqueror. In the
case of nations at war, the conqueror dictates the terms of peace; in
the case of subjects engaged in rebellion, when the rebellion is subdued, the government enforces or mitigates the penalty. The terms

of the conqueror in this case, or the penalties fixed by the government, are embodied in this proposed amendment. In either view of the case, there can be no disgrace incurred by the acceptance of the terms proposed, because they are proposed by a powerful government to the people of states disarmed and unable to resist its authority. The disqualifications proposed, practically, do not go to the army that surrendered at Appomattox courthouse. I suppose not five per cent. of the individuals who composed that army, will be affected by the proposed constitutional amendment. There were, perhaps, more able-bodied Virginians in the state, who were detailed or exempted in one way or another from military service, than were bearing arms on that day. The disqualifications will fall chiefly on this class. They ought not to complain, because they did not expose their persons in the strife to secure victor in a war they so largely contributed to inaugurate. There were few at Appomattox who had been active in bringing on the war.

The pardon issued by the President assumed that severe pains and penalties had been incurred by the individual receiving it, and required an acknowledgment by the recipient that he had committed the offence. Congress, also, declares that the offence was committed, and affixes the disqualifications imposed upon certain offenders as a mitigated penalty. The pardons of the President were eagerly sought, and accepted with professions of gratitude. It cannot be contended that no disgrace attaches to the acknowledgment of a wrong where forgiveness is promised, and that it would be dishonorable to acknowledge the same fault where the consequences of the admission merely go to the disqualification from holding office.

But are the conditions imposed by congress hard? Congress indicated that the disabilities enumerated in the amendment are not to be perpetual, by reserving to itself the power to repeal them. The conditions are not nearly as hard as they might be. The person of the citizen is safe; his property is not threatened with confiscation; it is not proposed to administer our laws by strangers; the power over the question of suffrage is left with the states. For the sake of securing peace and its blessings, may it not be an act of exalted patriotism for a portion of the old and the middle-aged citizens to yield gracefully to a necessity they cannot avert? It only brings the young men a little earlier into public life, and will tend to the earlier development of their energies. By the acceptance of the amendment tranquility will be secured to the South. The young men and the old men will enter upon a new field of prosperity; intercommunications will be opened between all parts of the country, and by the exercise of a little forbearance, in a few years a perfect restoration will be effected.

But it is proposed to reject the amendment and abide events; and the question is frequently asked, what will be the result? The answer is involved in doubt. The condition of the country is unsettled, and there will be no tranquility until the status of the unrepresented states is fixed. I have no means of knowing what the action of congress will be, in the event of the rejection of the amendment. It seems to me most probable, that it will be claimed, that through illegal interference by the President in the unrepresented states, the political power of those states, has been placed in the hands of those who were lately in rebellion against the government, and who withhold political power from those who were and are loyal to the government of the United States; that they refuse to comply with the requirements of congress, to entitle them to representation, and are, therefore, still, practically, in rebellion against the government; and that the loyal people of these states are thus deprived of a representation in the councils of the nation. Congress will be asked to set aside the state organizations created by the President, and place these states under the control of loyal men, who will accept such conditions as may be imposed by congress. If congress should adopt this course, the President has no power to resist it, because if adopted by two-thirds of each house, it will be the law of the land.

Virginia would not be liable to this condition of things; but I have treated the subject as though she were in the same condition with the states re-organized by the President—first, because I know that your action will have an important influence over these states; and secondly, because as we are now unrepresented, we will have, in effect, to conform to the same conditions imposed on those states, which will in all probability be much more objectionable to our people, than the amendment now proposed; for when a constitutional amendment shall be adopted by the requisite number of states, whatever disqualifications are created thereby, will be enforced by stringent laws of congress.

The amendment is now before you for ratification or rejection. I have endeavored to make a fair and full statement to you, in regard to this whole subject, as it presents itself to my mind.

Gentlemen, other topics will engage your attention. I have only alluded to such as I conceive to be important to the welfare of the commonwealth. I leave the whole subject with you, devoutly imploring the blessing of Divine Providence for your guidance and protection, with the hope that wisdom and forbearance may characterize all your deliberations.

F. H. PEIRPOINT.

Richmond, December 3, 1866.

Document 3

ABILITY OF THE STATE OF VIRGINIA TO MAINTAIN
PUBLIC EDUCATION.

The gross annual production of one and a quarter millions
of people like ours, with four hundred millions of dollars'
worth of property, is immense; but, vast as it is, it is all consumed—not that it is all destroyed and lost, but it is made use
of one way or another; and, a term of years being considered,
everything in the whole country is consumed, except the land
and the most substantial permanent improvements, and even
they are partially consumed.

But how is everything consumed? In just two ways: partly
by being reinvested for increase of value—partly by being used
for the gratification of desire, and thus permanently lost.
Necessary expenditures for the support of the producing population, and for carrying on every sort of productive business,
are all forms of reinvestment for future profit.

It is not so obvious, but equally true, that to this class also
belongs the support of the government, it being an investment
for the sake of that security of persons and property which is
an indispensable condition of production.

Public officers are the agents of society, employed to attend
to those interests which are common to all; and the work is
much better and more economically done by this method than
if the people were to undertake to do it for themselves.

An undue multiplication of public officers is, of course, to be
avoided; but, as a general rule, it is good economy to commit
all interests which are common to all to the hands of men who
may give special attention thereto, and thus allow the people
generally the opportunity of devoting themselves to their
strictly private affairs.

The multiplication of officers is a form of that division of
labor which the experience of the world has shown to be conducive to the success of all large operations. Whenever the
value of the time spent by private citizens in attending to a
matter of public interest is greater than the cost of an officer
to attend to it, the appointment of such an officer is good
economy, and therefore an investment for the sake of greater

profit: and it may be remarked, also, that the larger the pay given to such officer, the greater economy up to the point of securing the greatest ability and efficiency.

To the same class belong all forms of public or private expenditure, which return an amount of solid advantage greater in value than the amount expended.

But the other class of expenditures is very different in character and results from the one just considered. It is the consumption of the capital of the country for the mere gratification of desire, which amounts to its total destruction. And to this class belongs every form or degree of expenditure which cannot be called, in familiar phrase, "a paying investment;" in other words, every expenditure which is not necessary for the support and increased efficiency of the people, and for the economical conduct of really productive employment. In using the term "expenditure," reference is not made primarily or chiefly to the expenditure of money, but rather to the consumption of articles which it has cost money and labor to produce. Now, be it observed, that if these articles are used in such a way that their value is destroyed, as in the consumption of all luxuries, *then the country is just that much poorer*—just to that extent has she, in an economical point of view, been squandering her income, and in the production or purchase of those articles just that much labor and capital has been thrown away.

Before the subject was sounded to the bottom, it was the view of some political economists that if the luxuries were produced in the country, the purchase of them supported the producers, and thus contributed to the general wealth of the country; but the error of such, arose from confounding money with wealth. Money, by its purchasing power, represents wealth, but it is not itself wealth. Coin has a certain intrinsic value which, to that extent, may deserve the name, but beyond that, money is not wealth. Wealth consists in that which money buys—some sort of property, or rather product—and hence the destruction of commodities is the destruction of wealth.

Luxuries produced in a State and sold elsewhere may increase the wealth of the State by bringing back useful commodities, or money, which may be needed for the production of useful commodities at home. But so far as luxuries are consumed in a State, whether produced there or imported, in exchange for home productions, the capital, or solid wealth, of the State is thereby reduced to that extent.

Now, in probably almost every civilized State in the world, (and ours is not an exception), the annual destruction of wealth in the gratification of individual desire is many times greater than all the demands of the commonwealth; that is to say, in almost every State (including our own) the people are wasting, often to their serious detriment, far more than is needed by the government for all useful purposes.

I have endeavored to form some estimate of the amount of wealth consumed, without return, in Virginia, and although the sources of information fail to furnish exact figures, the indications are that it does not fall short of $20,000,000 per annum. It is not affirmed that all this expenditure is improper, but only that it is a destruction of wealth. The annual consumption in Virginia of alcoholic liquors alone must be near $19,000,000. The sales of liquors in the United States during the fiscal year ending June 30th, 1871, it has been calculated by Edward Young, the chief of the Bureau of Statistics, amounted to six hundred millions of dollars. This total is made up as follows: Sixty million gallons of whiskey, at six dollars a gallon, *retail*, $360,000,000. Two and a half million gallons of imported spirits, at ten dollars a gallon, $25,000,000. Ten million seven hundred thousand gallons of imported wine, at five dollars a gallon, $53,500,000. Six million five hundred thousand barrels of ale, beer, and porter, at twenty dollars a barrel, $130,000,000. Native brandies, wines, and cordials, in unknown quantities, have been consumed, involving, it is estimated, an expenditure of $31,500,000. These figures, although not so large as some that have been published, yet give a total that should astonish the consumers of ardent spirits. They give an annual consumption of about sixteen dollars' worth of spirits to every man, woman and child in the United States. If the Virginia people be average consumers, the amount expended in Virginia is $19,000,000 per annum. This, of course, includes what is used for medicine; but probably ninety-nine one-hundredths of it is used as a beverage, which,

in the eye of political economy, is a destruction of that much
of the wealth of the State. If to the loss of wealth directly, is
added the waste of time, neglect of business, injury to health,
disturbance of public order, and many other individual losses,
what a frightful tax it is upon the wealth of the State.

The consumption of tobacco is another expenditure which
political economy must class under the head of waste. The
tax paid to the United States on tobacco in Virginia last year
was $4,363,911. One-thirtieth of this is supposed, by one of the
revenue officers, to be consumed in Virginia. Besides this,
there is a considerable consumption of imported segars and
tobacco, so that the annual consumption is something like
$300,000, probably more.

There are a great many other wasteful expenditures of less
importance, but which would present a large aggregate, if
brought together. Could we sum up the amounts which are
carried off by theatricals, circuses, operas, lottery dealers, gift
enterprises, jugglers, and other exhibitors, gamblers, and
swindlers of all sorts, we should no doubt find that the people
of the State are expending several hundred thousand dollars on
these indulgences. Add to this what is spent in confectionery,
ornaments, costly furniture and equipage, expensive apparel,
and the amount would be enlarged by some hundreds of thousands more. Could we gather exact statistics on these and
other like expenditures, there is very little doubt that the grand
total would not be less than $20,000,000.

The right of persons to indulge themselves in these luxuries
is not called in question; but it is scarcely consistent in a
people to doubt their ability to educate the children of the
State, and to pay interest on their public debt, when they are
wastefully consuming five times as much as would do both.
The term "commonwealth" indicates the community of property and interest among the people of a State. It is only a
family, as to matters of this sort. What would be thought of
a family claiming to be too poor to educate the children and
pay its debts, whilst at the same time it is squandering far more
than would be needed for both?

The destruction of wealth by dogs has long been observed,
though never very accurately calculated. It is estimated by

the statistician connected with the Department of Agriculture at Washington, that there are five millions of dogs in the United States. Our share of these animals must be something like 160,000. Some newspaper writer estimates the food consumed by a dog as being sufficient to keep a hog. It is not uncommon for wealthy people in large cities to put their dogs in the country to be boarded, at certain seasons of the year. The price of dog-board among Pennsylvania farmers, some years ago, was from two to three dollars per month—at the rate, say, of thirty dollars per year for each dog. Of course, there was a profit in this; but probably the actual cost was not less than twelve dollars a year. This would be little over three cents a day; even the rough food thrown to them would be worth that, for chicken or pig feed. Take off two dollars, and suppose the cost to be ten dollars each, then the total cost of keeping the dogs in Virginia would be about $1,600,000 per annum. Were the cost but five dollars each, what a destruction of food for the very small value received! But dogs are not mere consumers—they are destroyers. Their ferocity and liability to madness produce great mental disquiet, to say nothing of the injuries they inflict upon persons. It is estimated, at the Agricultural Department, that the killing and maiming of sheep by dogs in the United States inflicts damages amounting to $2,000,000 annually. In this damage, Virginia has shared largely. But this constitutes only a small part of the injury to the sheep interest by dogs. The risk incurred is so great as to increase the cost of sheep-raising, and to deter many from entering upon a business which, but for that, would be peculiarly suited to the present condition of Virginia lands. In some States a tax is laid upon dogs, for the support of public schools.

On the facts and principles which have been adduced, the following conclusions may fairly be based:—

1. As long as within a State there is annual waste of income in amount far greater than is wanted for the education of the children of the State, poverty cannot fairly be plead as a reason for neglecting that duty. If, by the diversion into the public treasury of one-tenth of the capital now annually going to waste, the education of the whole population could thereby be

provided for, who can doubt the economy of the operation? And how would the argument be strengthened if it were shown, as might easily be done, that the reduction of this waste would not only save for valuable public uses that amount of wealth, but would, in a still greater ratio, benefit those who are engaged in this wasting process, and render them far more efficient and productive members of the community !

2. A State in embarrassed circumstances, needs to pursue for its recovery exactly the course proper for an individual similarly situated, viz: to lessen waste and increase production. And when the public virtue is equal to the demand upon it, the people will cheerfully deny themselves and increase their exertions, rather than allow their State to fall short of fulfilling any of its duties. And when taxation is properly distributed, and bears a just relation to the real wants of the State, the people will adjust their private habits to suit the public necessities, and more industry, economy, and thoughtful calculation will pervade the community; and that which at first was a cross, heavy to be borne, proves a blessing. The change of habits, which was at first severe, and even humiliating, results in a degree of ultimate prosperity never attained before.

8. The expenditure for public education is simply one form in which the people of a State invest a portion of their capital, with a view to larger returns in the future; and when the matter is understood in all its bearings, the people consider this the best of all their investments. The money raised for the purpose is all expended within the State—it goes directly back to the pockets of the people; and in its rounds it has sowed all over the land precious seed, which will spring up and bear fruit, some thirty, some sixty, and some an hundred fold.

By such expenditure as this the State is not poorer, but far richer. It is like an expenditure for clover seed by a farmer, which makes a return far greater than the outlay. And the State which refuses to educate its children on the score of economy, pursues just the destructive policy of the farmer who will not expend enough to procure proper seeds, manures, implements and labor, but pursues what he calls the cheap system of farming, which ends in the utter impoverishment of the land and its owner.

Let Virginia refuse to educate her people, and she will certainly never pay her public debt, because her ability to pay will not increase as fast as her debt will grow, until, like a hard worked but underfed beast of burden, she is crushed by the load. But let the invigorating influence of education permeate her masses, and by the force of her awakened energies she will bear her burdens lightly, and gather strength as she goes.

DISCUSSION OF THE PUBLIC SCHOOL SYSTEM.

The public school system ought to rest on a better foundation than the demands of a Constitution reluctantly accepted, or even on the will of a numerical majority. If after careful scrutiny it does not commend itself to the substantial, enlightened part of the community, it ought not to be continued permanently. It is not just, it is not for the public good, that the men who own the land, who wield the capital, who head the business enterprises of the State, should long continue under a policy which they regard as injurious and oppressive, and this, not only because they pay the chief part of the taxes, but because upon their cheerful energy the interests of all depend. Many of this important class of our citizens are now friendly to the cause; but in order that they may generally become not only the friends, but the determined supporters of the system, it is only needful that they be made fully acquainted with its advantages. Owing to peculiar circumstances, the subject of public free education, although frequently introduced, has never been fully discussed before the people of Virginia, so that many of our most worthy citizens have not had the opportunity of seriously considering the reasoning and testimony by which it is supported. It seems therefore proper for me, as the official head of the system, to embrace such opportunities as the present to exhibit views of the strong foundations on which the system rests. These views cannot all be presented in a single report: only a few leading topics are selected for discussion on the present occasion.

SOME REMARKS ON MORAL TRAINING.

The few points which I shall hereinafter argue in this report
are not those on which education has in past ages commonly
rested its claims upon mankind—not those which, in the large
view, are most worthy of consideration; but they are such as
belong appropriately to discussions on the utility of education
as a civil interest, and such as are specially suited to our present condition as a State. Education is commonly valued for
the benefit accruing to the individual receiving it; it is prosecuted by the State on account of its politico-economical advantages. But, in dwelling chiefly upon the public advantages of
education, I do not wish to be understood as undervaluing those
higher considerations connected with the personal well-being of
those who receive education; nor do I wish to be understood as
placing considerations of public policy above the motives of
parental and religious obligation. No form of obligation can
equal that resting upon parents and churches, who must concern themselves primarily with the interests of the children
themselves. Each of these three parties—the parents, the State
and the Church—is capable of conducting some particular part
of the child's education better than either of the others; but
this is not the place to define their respective provinces.

It is now generally admitted that the State cannot properly
teach religion. The reasons against her doing so are conclu-
sive, but need not now be given. It does not follow, however,
that all incidental allusions or observances of a religious character should be forbidden. Where they can be introduced in
an edifying and inoffensive way they should not be objected to;
but the true theory of civil government forbids the use of State
money or State authority in any way that contravenes individual rights of conscience. This whole controversy about the
use of the Bible in public schools is greatly to be deprecated.
It is damaging to the interests of both education and religion.
The time will come when a great deal of moral and religious
truth will be taught in the public schools, not theologically but
educationally. There is a religious common law accepted by
everybody, which will yet be embodied in text-books, and

taught in every school without offence. It is not dogmatic religion in any full sense, but it comprises cardinal religious doctrines, and a complete code of the highest and purest morality; and men of all creeds and characters in our land acknowledge in some form the authority of this religious common law. The existence and government of God constitutes its great controlling feature, and from that is developed the whole code of moral duties. The power of these higher obligations in forming the character of the young, and in controlling men through life, has been recognized in every age and nation. The fact that Mr. Huxley, a distinguished sceptic, is now endeavoring to compel the reading of the Bible in the public schools of England, furnishes only another addition to the multitudes of cases in which persons without a religious faith have testified to the disciplinary value of the teachings of the Scriptures.

Governor B. Gratz Brown, of Missouri, in an address of welcome to the National Teachers' Association, which met in St. Louis last August, touched upon an idea worthy of serious consideration. In commenting upon the propriety of enlarging the moral element in public teaching, he suggested the use of the criminal code as an instrument of moral education. These are his words:

"Apart from direct moral training, the best remedy will be found in taking the criminal code into your schools, and collating the action with the retribution; in demonstrating virtue as its own best reward, not by axiom but by illustration, and in showing forth by suitable methods that wrong is ever miscalculation, and therefore foreign to the first law of education. Have you to-day any text-book of crime and misdemeanor in your schools? Do your young grow up knowing what obtaining money under false pretences means? Are your lessons of the penitentiary and of the reformatory ever applied in the school-room? And yet whilst forcing the faculties of youth to their highest acuteness, you would leave them unguarded amid sordid greed for gain, and unschooled in the principles of honor and integrity."

This suggestion of Governor Brown's is in the right direction.

The common and statutory law of the land really contain the
materials out of which might be constructed a good system of
religious ethics. How much pure morality and even elevated
religious teaching may be found in the pages of Blackstone!
It is true that the penalties of civil law are physical rather than
moral, but there is something very impressive in these severe
judgments of society against immorality. And in truth it is a
question whether men are not more governed by fear and by
the power of public sentiment, than by a sense of duty.

But in addition to the doctrines of the civil code, should be
inculcated the principles of what may be called the social code,
which requires not merely the observance of public law, but of
all those private obligations, which are none the less important
and binding because they are not or cannot be embodied in
legislative enactments—obligations which can only be enforced
by the power of a resistless public sentiment. The duties of
citizenship should also be a part of public instruction. It is
just for the want of this sort of teaching that in so many parts
of the country official corruption is allowed such opportunity,
and such impunity. The existence of so much corruption
evinces not only a want of moral tone among voters, but a want
of that sort of moral perspicacity which comes from the exercise of the moral faculty in that particular direction. There is
probably in all our American States a sufficient substratum of
moral honesty to purify the public service if it were only enlightened and trained. Our political salvation must come from
that direction. Our State has been wonderfully preserved so
far from public corruption, and is now in a condition for har-
monious action. The moral worth of a State was never more
united and powerful than it is in Virginia to-day. Shall it not
demand that the youth of the land shall be so educated in every
right principle, that they shall issue from the schools fully
rounded in character, and well equipped morally as well as men-
tally for all the duties of citizenship? Of course, the reference
here is only to those simple principles of morality and those
fundamental duties of citizenship which are accepted by all parties and individuals alike, preserving a broad line between this
and party politics on the one hand, and sectarianism in religion
on the other.

But whilst the public school system may be improved by the introduction of more direct moral teaching, its moral tendencies, even as it is now conducted, are in the right direction. The evils consequent upon being without such a system, are far greater than any which are attendant upon it, because the evils of ignorance are far greater than those of even the most purely intellectual education. The general moral and religious tone of a public school is usually the same as characterizes the neighborhood in which it is situated. If there is good salt around it, the school will not remain unseasoned. A teacher of suitable character is constantly exercising a good influence upon the pupils by both example and precept; and, in a country like ours, almost every text-book prepared for elementary schools has a vein of moral and religious truth running through it. But supposing (what is never true) that the children never received any directly moral or religious instruction at school, there is time enough for imparting such instruction elsewhere. There are 168 hours in a week, and only 30 of those hours are spent by children in the school-room. If they have parents and others who can teach them moral and religious truth, there is abundant opportunity for so doing; but if, unfortunately, they have none to care for their souls at home, it is far better that they should be provided with the means of deriving good from other sources, than they should be left under the evil influence of ignorance and impiety. They will thus be introduced to the current literature of the times, in which wholesome sentiments largely prevail, and thus they will be rendered fitter subjects for evangelization. One of the great hindrances to the progress of the Gospel is found in the ignorance of the people. They do not profit by the services of the sanctuary. In many neighborhoods also, the time of Sunday school teachers is largely taken up with teaching scholars to read, when they should employ all their precious moments in teaching the children those things which may make them wise unto salvation. In a few years it will be found that the public schools have doubled the power of the Sunday schools, and greatly increased the power of the pulpit.

In the *Princeton Review* of Jan. 1871, Dr. Bittinger thus states

the true doctrine on this subject in an able article entitled,
"Responsibility of society for the causes of crime":

"Ignorance is a source of crime. It operates in various
ways: first, to expose men to it, and then to prepare them for
it. The uncultivated mind is weakened by non-use. For lack
of ideas it is often left to the suggestions of the animal appe-
tites, with their debasing and corrupting tendencies. In a land
of books and schools, ignorance is not consistent with self-
respect or manliness. Even the pitiable standard set up in our
prison statistics—to be able to read—is far above many of the
adults that enter their walls. But when we erect the higher
and truer one—of being able to read with facility and zest—
such proficiency as puts knowledge, both as a pastime and a
power, within men's reach, how beggarly is the show then
among our prison population! The average per cent. of the
State prison population of New York, in 1864, that could not
read was 32. Now, admitting that the remainder could read,
and not disparaging the quality of it, it shows eleven times
more ignorance among these twenty-four hundred inmates than
among the whole outside adult population of the State. Of
those outside the penitentiaries, only three per cent. could not
read, while 32 per cent. of those inside could not. Even not
knowing how to read is eleven times more likely to lead to
crime than knowing; or, as Dr. Wines has put it, one-third of
the crime is committed by one-fiftieth of the population. So
great is the affinity of crime for ignorance. Ninety-seven per
cent. of the non-prison population of New York, in 1864, could
read; in the same year only sixty-eight per cent. of the prison
population could read. Knowing how to read is two-thirds as
favorable to honesty as not knowing: in other words, knowledge
is more preventive of crime than promotive of virtue.

"But as the want of practical knowledge is as really ignorance as the want of book-knowledge, the following figures by
Mr. Byers, late chaplain of the Ohio Penitentiary, are more to
the point as to the influence of ignorance upon crime. Out of
2,120 under his care, 67 per cent. were uneducated, that is, men
who could barely read, or who could merely scratch their
names; 14 per cent. did not know their "A B C's;" 74 per cent.

had never learned a trade. Here we have 81 per cent. ignorant of books, and 74 per cent. ignorant of a trade. Apply these proportions to the outside population, and what a mass of ignorance and helplessness it would make!"

The percentage of illiteracy in the European prisons is much higher. Mr. Kay's English statistics place the rate as high as 95 per cent. among the convicts, and show that not one criminal in two hundred has what deserves to be called an education.

The infidel tendencies charged upon public schools do not exist. Modern heresy and scepticism are indeed found closely allied with intelligence, but it is not with the simple intelligence of the popular mind which is everywhere true to the faith. The sources of infidelity are to be found in the temples, not in the synagogues, of learning. Germany originates all manner of sceptical philosophies, yet the Germans are the greatest church-goers in the world.

Before passing to views more especially suitable to a State paper, I will introduce an extract from the *Princeton Review* in confirmation of my last remark. It is taken also from the January number, 1871, and the author is Rev. Dr. Hodge, than whom a higher authority does not exist on the continent:

"Prussia, if judged by her institutions and laws, must be regarded as the most thoroughly Christian nation in the world. As the Prussian system secures that every man shall be a soldier, so it secures that every man shall be a Christian, so far as knowledge and profession are concerned. No child, although barefooted, of twelve years of age, can be found in Berlin or Halle who cannot read and write, and who is not familiar with Scripture history. The experiment has been often made. The children are all required to go to school. The pastors are required to devote so many hours a week to their religious instruction. The churches are all free, and whatever may be the character of the sermons, the Scriptures are read, an evangelical liturgy is used, and devout hymns are sung. The hymnology of Germany is probably richer than that of any other Christian people, if not than that of all other nations combined. The Germans are a musical people, and these hymns are sung not only in the churches, but in the homes of the poor all over the land. Hence, while the French soldiers are roused by the Marseillaise, the Germans nerve themselves by singing the grand old hymn of Luther, 'A sure defence is our God, a trusty shield and weapon.' The churches throughout Prussia, as a general thing, are crowded with worshippers. The rich and titled may or may not be there in curtained stalls, but the body of the church is thronged by the common people. While, therefore, in Prussia, as elsewhere, many of the educated, and especially of the scientific class, have given themselves up to scepticism, the nation, as a nation, is eminently Christian."

*   *   *

PUBLIC EDUCATION IN VIRGINIA.

Much sport is made of the reply which Governor Berkeley gave in 1670 to the English commissioners, who addressed to him inquiries as to the condition of the colonies: "I thank God there are no free schools, nor printing, and I hope we shall not have these hundred years;" but Governor Berkeley was not a fair representative of the Virginia spirit in any respect. It is true, that neither schools nor printing flourished in the colony at that period; but provision was made for public education almost cotemporaneously with the original settlement of the country. The first movement contemplated the establishment of a college for the education of Indians. Its plan was subsequently enlarged, and the location for it made on the north bank of the James, just above what is now known as Dutch Gap. Holmes, in his Annals of America, vol. 1, p. 157, gives the following account of it:

"The King of England having formerly issued his letters patent to the several Bishops of the kingdom for collecting money to erect a college in Virginia for the education of Indian children, nearly £1,500 had been already paid toward this benevolent and pious design, and Henrico had been selected as a suitable place for the seminary. The Virginia Company, on the recommendation of Sir Edwin Sandys, its treasurer, now granted 10,000 acres of land, to be laid off for the University of Henrico. This donation, while it embraced the original object, was intended also for the foundation of a seminary of learning for the English."

But Henrico College was to have a feeder. Provision was made for a great *free school* in 1621, one year after the Mayflower had touched Plymouth Rock, and twenty-two years before New England began her educational system. The early free school movement in Virginia is mentioned by most of the historians, and is thus described in Holmes's Annals, vol. 1, p. 173:

"A free school was founded in Virginia. An East India ship having returned from India to England, the ship's company, incited by the example and persuasions of Mr. Copeland, their chaplain, contributed £70 toward building a church or a free school in that colony. Thirty pounds more were given by one unknown person, and £25 were afterwards added by another. An unknown person also gave forty shillings, yearly, for a sermon before the society. Many excellent religious books, of the value of £10, and a very valuable map of all that coast of America, were also sent by a person unknown for the college at Henrico. Mr. Thomas Bargrave, a preacher at that place, gave a library, valued at one hundred marks; and the inhabitants made a contribution of £1,500, to build a house for the entertainment of strangers. It was determined to build a free school in Charles City, which was thought to be most convenient to all parts of the colony, and it was named *The East India School*. The company allotted, for the maintenance of the master and usher, 1,000 acres of land, with five servants and an overseer. This school was to be collegiate, and to have dependence on the college at Henrico, into which, as soon as the college should be sufficiently endowed, and capable of receiving students, pupils were to be admitted and advanced according to their deserts and proficiency in learning."

But these liberal schemes came to a sad termination the very
next year in consequence of the great massacre of the colo-
nists by the Indians under Opechancanough. The cause of
education thus received a check, from which it only began to
recover, when, thirty-nine years later, William & Mary College
was founded.

The duty of providing the means of education from public
funds has, however, never been seriously called in question in
our State. So far as there have been differences among our
legislators, they have been not concerning the principle involved, but as to the mode and extent of applying the principle.
It will be seen by the following brief sketch that, coëval with our
independence, the Legislature of Virginia gave special consideration to the subject of popular education. Previous to the
Revolutionary War, several of our Virginia statesmen had
cherished a great admiration for the institutions of New England. Considering the moral chasm which now exists between
the sections, one is amazed, who now reads for the first time
the strong language of approval which such men as Patrick
Henry and Richard Bland Lee employed in commending the
peculiarities of the New England system in that day. Thomas
Jefferson imbibed so deep a conviction of the value of the
public school system then in vogue in New England, that he
gave all his powers to secure its full adoption by the State of
Virginia. In 1779, in the midst of the war, Mr. Jefferson and
George Wythe, as members of a committee, made a report to
the Legislature embodying this system of education. The
Legislature finally adopted Mr. Jefferson's system in 1796, but
inserted a provision allowing each county court to declare when
the system should go into operation within the limits of its
jurisdiction. This proviso was the means of defeating the
plan; for at that time the county courts were in unfriendly
hands.

But Mr. Jefferson's zeal in the cause never flagged. As late
as 1820, in writing to Joseph C. Cabell, Esq., he uses this language:—

" Surely, Governor Clinton's display of the gigantic effort of
New York toward the educating of her citizens will stimulate

. the pride as well as the patriotism of *our Legislature* to look to the reputation and safety of our country, to rescue it from the degradation of becoming the Barbary of the Union, * * * To that condition it is fast sinking."

But the Legislature of Virginia has in her State policy given preference to internal improvements over popular education; yet it has never at any period been wholly indifferent to the educational wants of the people. As early as 1810 an act was passed which founded the State "Literary Fund," which grew by accretion, until at the opening of the late war it had nearly reached the sum of $2,000,000. The proceeds of this fund were designed to be used exclusively for common-school education. Its original nucleus consisted of fines, forfeitures, and escheats. To this was added the debt due to Virginia from the United States, for claims connected with the Revolutionary war and the war of 1812.

In 1811, one year after the creation of the Literary Fund, an act was passed concerning the Fund, containing the following preamble :—

" Whereas, it is provided that the Literary Fund shall be appropriated to the sole benefit of schools to be kept in each and every county in this Commonwealth, an object equally humane, just, and necessary, involving alike the interests of humanity and the preservation of the Constitution, laws and liberty of the good people of this Commonwealth, the present General Assembly solemnly protest against any other application of the said funds by any succeeding General Assembly to any other object than the education of the poor."

In 1819, and afterward for some years, $45,000 was annually divided among the counties from this Fund. In 1821, the then incipient University began to receive $15,000 *per annum* from this Fund, and the appropriation continued until some time during the late war. By the year 1849 the sum divided among the counties was $70,000, and by 1860 the Fund was yielding $80,000 for apportionment. For some years previously the Military Institute had received $1,500 annually from this Fund.

The Fund has yielded nothing since the war, as is elsewhere stated.

Mr. Jefferson's plan, as embodied in the act of 1796, had in it the elements of a thorough free school system for the free population. It provided that in each county three school trustees should be chosen by the people. These officers were called "aldermen," and were clothed with plenary powers. They were to estimate the amount needed for supplying the people with free schools in their respective counties, and it was made the duty of the sheriff to raise the amount by tax on property. The schools were called in this act simply "public schools." Information is wanting as to the action of counties in regard to this law; but the system certainly made but little, if any, progress in the State, and the law became a dead letter for the reason heretofore given.

Before passing from this school act, it is worth while to call attention to the sentiments adopted in those days by the Legislature of Virginia. In the preamble of the act of 1796 occurs these words :—

"Whereas, upon a review of· the history of mankind, it seemeth that—however favorable republican government, founded on the principles of equal liberty, justice and order, may be to human happiness—no real stability or lasting permanency thereof can be rationally hoped for, if the minds of the citizens be not rendered liberal and humane, and be not fully impressed with the importance of those principles from whence those blessings proceed : With a view, therefore, to lay the first foundations of a system of education, which may tend to produce those desirable purposes," &c.

The act of Assembly of 1810 struck the educational idea which proved to be the most acceptable to the ruling classes in Virginia, and which, although wholly unsatisfactory in operation, was pertinaciously adhered to for fifty years. It has commonly been spoken of as the "*pauper system*," because only the children of the indigent received any benefit. The support of the system came entirely from the Literary Fund. Each county.

court was required to appoint from five to fifteen school commissioners, who, at first, were not allowed to use the money
apportioned for any purpose but paying the tuition of poor
children in primary schools. About the year 1849 they were
allowed to expend five per cent. of the money for the purchase
of books, and other contingencies; and any unexpended
balance might be contributed to the support of poor young
men in academies or colleges, in the counties where the surplus
might occur. The clerk of the board of school commissioners,
for taking the census of children, and other official services,
might receive a salary not exceeding ten dollars a year! The
other commissioners received nothing. Finding that the system had not been very vigorously administered, the school
commissioners were instructed by law to appoint an officer of
great possibilities, known as " county superintendent of
schools." A very proper list of duties was assigned to the
officer; and in order that the services of a competent man
might be secured, and he be stimulated to an euergetic discharge of his duties, he was made treasurer of the money apportioned to his county, and allowed to retain five per cent. of
the money he disbursed, which gave him an income of fully
twenty-five dollars a year; except in the smaller counties,
where he got less!

As an illustration of the economy of the " cheap method" of
managing great public interests, it is worth while to call attention to a diminution which the Literary Fund suffered at one
period of its history. The funds sent to the counties were so
carelessly managed, and the reports were so erroneous, that a
series of errors crept into the books of the Auditor, which
caused a serious reduction in the amount of the Literary Fund.
This was brought to the attention of the Legislature in 1822,
and an act was passed with a view to securing more care and
system in the management of the funds. Then, for the first
time, were uniform blank forms furnished to the school officers
for accounts and reports.

By means of the " pauper system," a large number of poor
children received the rudiments of an education, who would
otherwise have remained totally illiterate; but the system could
not be regarded as even a tolerable substitute for a general sys-

tem of education. It has passed away forever, and let it be dismissed with the single remark, that no system of education, based upon a discrimination between poor people and others, can ever be made to harmonize with the institutions or public sentiment of our country, and no set of poorly paid officers will ever give efficiency to any system.

But besides the great " pauper system," and besides certain special acts for particular counties, the Legislature of 1845–'6 adopted a " Free school system," which any county had liberty to adopt by a vote of the people. The only particularly good feature in this system was, that the County Board of School Commissioners fixed the amount needed for the support of schools in the county, and the court, or town council, was required to order the necessary levy. Several counties adopted the system, but with what results I have not been able to ascertain particularly. My impression is, that it was not generally successful. It could not have had any high degree of success, worked as it was by officers, whose remuneration was a mere trifle, whilst the duties to be performed were numerous, and indispensable to success.

But these different schemes of public education, although partial and unsatisfactory, demonstrate the truth of my declaration, that Virginia has from the beginning admitted the propriety and duty of the State's making provision for the education of her people. And I have chosen this recital of facts, not only as being interesting, but as being perhaps the most effective way of disposing of those objections to the public free school system, which are founded on its alleged agrarianism. The Virginia Legislature has not in the past been impressed with objections of that sort, and probably will not be in the future. As heretofore remarked, the only controversy which has ever existed has been as to what should be the framing of the school system, whether it should be partial or general, if general, whether by counties or by the State. The experience of the State, with former systems, will tend to render the present mode stable.

BASIC FACTS

Capital City .... Richmond

Nickname .... The Old Dominion

Flower .... Dogwood

Bird .... Cardinal

Tree .... Dogwood

Song .... *Carry Me Back to Old Virginia*

Animal .... Fox Hound

Entered the Union .... June 25, 1788

STATISTICS*

Land Area (square miles) 39,780
    Rank in Nation 36th

Population† 4,765,000
    Rank in Nation 13th
    Density per square mile 119.8

Number of Representatives in Congress 10

Capital City .... Richmond
    Population 249,431
    Rank in State 2nd

Largest City .... Norfolk
    Population 307,951

Number of Cities over 10,000 Population 30

Number of Counties 96

---

* Based on 1970 census statistics compiled by the Bureau
of the Census.
† Estimated by Bureau of the Census for July 1, 1972.

VIRGINIA

MAP OF CONGRESSIONAL DISTRICTS
OF VIRGINIA

SELECTED BIBLIOGRAPHY

A huge collection of reference materials exists on all phases of Virginia history and development. The following is a highly selective cross-section of such publications. Special attention should be called to the special booklet studies of Jamestown 350th Anniversary Studies, the Jamestown Essays on Representation, and the current publications of the Virginia Independence Bicentennial Commission.

Ambler, Charles H. Sectionalism in Virginia from 1776 to 1861 (Chicago, 1910)

Barbour, Philip L., Pocahontas and Her World (Boston, 1970)

Bemiss, Samuel, The Three Charters of the Virginia Company (Jamestown, 1957)

Bridenbaugh, Carl, Seat of Empire: The Political Role of Eighteenth Century Williamsburg (Charlottesville, 1963)

Bruce, Philip A., Institutional History of Virginia in the Seventeenth Century (Gloucester, Mass., 1964)

-----Economic History of Virginia in the Seventeenth Century (Gloucester, Mass., 1935)

-----Social Life in Virginia in the Seventeenth Century (Richmond, 1907)

Buck, J. L. Blair, The Development of Public Schools in Virginia, 1607-1952 (Richmond, 1952)

Chamberlain, Samuel, Springtime in Virginia (New York, 1947)

Chandler, J. A. C., Representation in Virginia (Baltimore, 1896)

-----History of Suffrage in Virginia (Baltimore, 1901)

Dabney, Virginius, Virginia: The New Dominion (New York, 1971)

Davis, Richard B., Intellectual Life in Jefferson's Virginia (Chapel Hill, 1964)

Dowdey, Clifford, The Virginia Dynasties (Boston, 1969)

-----Experiment in Rebellion (Garden City, N.Y,, 1946)

Eckenrode, H. J., The Revolution in Virginia (Boston, 1916)

Fishwick, Marshall, Virginia: A New Look at the Old Dominion (New York, 1959)

Gottman, Jean, Virginia in Our Century (Charlottesville, 1969)

Grigsby, Hugh B., The Virginia Convention of 1776 (Rich-
    mond, 1855)
-----The Virginia Convention of 1829-30 (Richmond, 1854)
Lankford, John, ed., Captain John Smith's America: Se-
    lections from his Writings (New York, 1967)
Moger, Allen W., Virginia: Bourbonism to Byrd, 1870-1925
    (Charlottesville, 1968)
Moore, Virginia, Virginia is a State of Mind (New York,
    1942)
Morton, Richard L., Colonial Virginia (Chapel Hill, 1960)
Pearson, Charles C., The Readjustor Movement in Virginia
    (New Haven, 1917)
Rouse, Parke, Virginia and the English Heritage in America
    (New York, 1966)
Sheldon, William D., Populism in the Old Dominion
    (Princeton, 1935)
Swindler, William F., Government by the People: Theory
    and Reality in Virginia (Charlottesville, 1969)
Van Schreeven, William J., The Conventions and Constitu-
    tions of Virginia, 1776-1966 (Richmond, 1967)
Wertenbaker, Thomas J., The Shaping of Colonial Virginia
    (New York, 1958)
Wilkinson, J. Harvie III, Harry Byrd and the Changing
    Face of Virginia Politics, 1945-1966 (Charlottesville,
    1968)

NAME INDEX

This index includes names of individuals mentioned in the Chronology and in the portion of the Biographical Directory preceding the alphabetical list of members of Congress. For the latter, see pages

Almond, J. Lindsay, 28, 35
Andros, Edmund, 34
Argall, Samuel, 33
Arnold, Benedict, 14
Bacon, Nathaniel, 6
Bacon, Nathaniel (II), 33
Barbour, James, 17, 34
Barbour, Robert, 20
Battle, John S., 27, 35
Bennett, Richard, 33
Berkeley, Norbourne, 11, 34
Berkeley, William, 5-7, 33
Beverley, Robert, 7, 8
Blair, James, 7, 34
Bland, Richard, 11
Brooke, Robert, 16, 34
Brown, John, 20
Buchanan, James, 20, 26
Burr, Aaron, 17
Burwell, Lewis, 34
Byrd, Harry F., 26-28, 35
Byrd, William, II, 11
Cabell, William H., 16, 34
Cameron, William E., 24, 35
Campbell, David, 19, 34
Carrol, Charles, 19
Carter, James E., 30
Carter, Robert, 34
Charles I, 3
Chichele, Henry, 33
Clark, George Rogers, 13, 19
Cornwallis, Lord, 14
Cromwell, Oliver, 5
Craig, Robert, 20
Culpepper, Thomas, 33

Dale, Thomas, 2
Dalton, John, 31
Dalton, Theodore R., 28
Darden, Colgate, Jr., 27, 35
Davis, Jefferson, 22
Davis Westmoreland, 26, 35
de Grasse, le Compte, 15
Dickenson, John, 11
Digges, Edward, 33
Dinwiddie, Robert, 34
Drysdale, Hugh, 34
Elizabeth II, Queen, 30
Fauquier, Francis, 34
Floyd, John, 34, 18, 20
Ford, Gerald R., 30
Ford, Susan, 30
Gates, Thomas, 2, 33
George II, 9, 20
George III, 9
Giles, William B., 18, 34
Gilmer, Thoms W., 19, 34
Godwin, Mills, 28, 29, 35
Gooch, William, 34
Grant, Ulysses S., 22, 23
Gray, Garland, 28
Greene, Nathanael, 19
Gregory, John M., 34
Harrison, Albertis S., 28, 35
Harrison, Benjamin, 14, 34
Harvey, John, 4, 33
Hays, Anthony, 11
Henry, Patrick, 10, 12-13, 15, 34
Hirohito, Emperor, 30
Holliday, F.W.M., 23, 35
Holton, A. Linwood, 29, 35

147

Howard, Lord, 7, 33
Huntington, Collis P., 24
Jackson, Thomas (Stonewall), 21
James I, 1
Jefferson, Thomas, 13, 14, 16, 17, 18, 34
Jeffries, Herbert, 33
Jennings, Edmund, 34
Johnson, Joseph, 20, 34
Jones, Hugh, 9
Kemper, James L., 23, 34
Lee, Fitzhugh 24, 35
Lee, Henry, 16, 34
Lee, Richard Henry, 12, 13
Lee, Robert E., 21, 22
Lee, Thomas, 34
Letcher, John, 21, 34
Lincoln, Abraham, 22
Mackemie, Francis, 8
Madison, James, 17
Mahone, Richard, 23, 24
Mann, William H., 26, 35
Marshall, John, 16
Martin, Tom, 25, 26
Mary II, 7
Mason, George, 13
Matthews, Samuel, 5, 33
McDowell, James, 34
McKinney, Philip, 24, 35
Miller, Francis P., 27
Monroe, James, 16, 17, 18, 34
Montague, Andrew John, 25, 35
Murray, John, 11, 34
Nelson, Thomas, 14, 34
Nelson, William, 34
Newport, Christopher, 1
Nicholas, William C., 17, 34
Nicholson, Francis, 8, 34
Nott, Edward, 34
O'Ferrall, Charles T., 25, 35
Opechancanoe, 4
Page, John, 16, 34
Patton, John M., 34
Paul VI, Pope, 30
Peery, George C., 27, 35
Percy, George, 33
Pierpont, F.H., 21, 34
Pleasants, James, 18, 34
Pocahontas, 2
Poe, Edgar Allan, 19
Pollard, John Garland, 26, 27, 35

Pott, John, 33
Powhatan, 1, 2
Preston, James C., 17, 34
Price, George C., 27, 35
Randolph, Beverley, 15, 34
Randolph, Edmund, 15, 34
Randolph, Peyton, 12
Randolph, Peyton, (II), 17
Randolph, Thomas, 18, 34
Ratcliffe, John, 1, 33
Robertson, Wyndham, 19, 34
Rockefeller, John D., Jr., 27
Rolfe, John, 2
Rutherford, John, 34
Sadat, Anwar, 30
Scofield, John M., 22
Smith, Al, 27
Smith George W., 17, 34
Smith, John, 1
Smith, William, 20, 34
Somers, George, 2
Spencer, Nicholas, 33
Spong, William B., 28
Spottswood, Alexander, 8, 34
Stanley, Thomas B., 28, 35
Stuart, Alexander H. H., 22
Stuart, Henry C., 26, 35
Swanson, Claude A., 26, 35
Taylor, J. Hoge, 25, 35
Tazewell, Littleton W., 19, 34
Teach, Edward, 9
Trinkle, E. Lee, 26, 35
Tuck, William H., 27, 35
Turner, Nat, 19
Tyler, James, H., 25, 35,
Tyler, John, Jr., 18, 34
Tyler, John, Sr., 17, 34
Underwood, John R., 22
Walker, Gilbert C., 23, 34
Walton, M.L., 25
Washington, George, 10, 15, 16
Wells, Henry H., 22, 34
West, Francis, 33
West, Thomas, 2, 33
William III, 7
Wilson, Woodrow, 26
Wingate, Edward-Maria, 1, 33
Wise, Henry A., 20, 34
Wood, James, 16, 34
Wyatt, Francis, 4, 33
Yeardley, George, 33